EVANGELISTIC SERMONS THAT WORK!

An international evangelist shares six soul-winning sermons,
plus practical guidelines on evangelistic preaching.

Copyright

Published by Shockwave Creative
www.shockwaves.pro

Cover design by Peter Dunn
www.newcreation.com

Table of Contents

Acknowledgements

This book is dedicated to the huge number of people who have had an input, or any contribution, to my journey along the path of life that God prepared for me to this very day.

I particularly honour my amazing wife Agnes, who has been my rock in over 30 years of marriage and ministry. Also, my sons Peter, John, and Mark, I am so proud of you all and the Christian young men you have become. My late parents, "Paddy" and Rosemary, and my brother Stephen and his wife Heather, my sister Heather and her husband Michael, all deserve my deepest gratitude. My wife's late parents, Pat and Maureen Park, were also a great encouragement and blessing to me. I also honour the late world evangelist Aril Edvardsen (Norway) whose ministry had a profound impact upon me.

In addition, there is a huge list of friends, partners, co-workers, leaders, pastors, evangelists, churches, Bible school teachers, authors, and others who have all played a key role in helping me to this point in life. Many will be unaware of just what a part they have played, thank you all.

First and foremost, I dedicate this book to the Lord Jesus Christ, the one who saved my soul and has led me every step of the way. I pray that this book will encourage, inspire and uplift those who read it. I pray that preachers and ministers of the Gospel will be encouraged in their ministry, and see many souls come to a personal faith in Jesus Christ.

God bless you all,

Richard Gunning
May 2023

Foreword

I first met Richard Gunning over 20 years ago in Belfast, Northern Ireland at a special conference for evangelists. Richard had recently started a network for campaign evangelists called ACE (Association of Campaign Evangelists) and I had heard many good reports from friends and colleagues.

It was very clear to me, from the very first meeting, that Richard Gunning has a passionate desire to train and raise up young evangelists for the future. His desire to pass on his knowledge and experience made a deep impression on me as a young preacher of the Gospel. In addition, his willingness to take young preachers with him on his campaign trips was something that really resounded with my heart, as that was how I personally was propelled into ministry!

I have heard Richard preach the Gospel in different settings and his sermons are always simple, clear, and easy to understand. Above all, they lead the unsaved people to a point of making a decision to accept Jesus Christ as their Lord and Saviour. Whether it is in a remote village, a local church or a huge Gospel campaign, souls regularly come to the Lord after hearing Richard Gunning preach the Gospel.

I am sure that this book of proven, soul winning sermons, and practical advice, will be a help to many evangelists, both young and not so young!

May God bless you as you read this book.

Jonas Andersson
Chairman of the "Association of Campaign Evangelists" (ACE)
Director of "Go Out Mission," Sweden.

Nässjö, Sweden

April 2023

Introduction

I gave my life to Jesus Christ as a young man, aged 20 years old. My mother had given me a book late one night by the famous American evangelist **Billy Graham.** I read the book from cover to cover, and then felt a strong sense of conviction about my selfish and sinful life. I asked Jesus to come into my heart and change my life on 1st January 1977, this was the start of a new life where God started to shape and mould me, and eventually send me out as an **evangelist to the nations.**

In 1982 I learned the Norwegian language, and then travelled to Norway to go to a Bible school and studied missions and evangelism at *"Troens Bevis Bibel & Misjons Institutt"* (in English: "Evidence of Faith Bible & Missions Institute.") There I was greatly impacted by the life and **ministry of the late Evangelist Aril Edvardsen,** probably the greatest Christian evangelist ever to emerge from Scandinavia.

In 1990 I travelled to **Kenya** with my wife Agnes, and together with Pastor Peter Karangu we launched "Reach the Unreached Ministries," focusing our efforts on the unreached tribes and villages. After attending a campaign led by the late **Evangelist Reinhard Bonnke,** we started doing campaigns in regional towns.

Later the Lord opened doors for me to preach in many nations: India, Russia, Pakistan, Sudan, Ethiopia, Burkina Faso, Norway, Sweden, Finland, Denmark, and Ireland. You can read my life story in my autobiography, *"From Belfast to the Ends of the Earth"* which is available to buy on Amazon.

Giving opportunities to young evangelists has always been something close to my heart. I have taken many young preachers with me on mission trips and helped them to get started in ministry. **This book is born out of that desire to help young evangelists.** This book contains sermons I have used over many years, they are simple but effective, anyone can understand them. They are simple Gospel messages that lead the unsaved people to a point where they understand their need of Jesus, and thousands upon thousands have accepted Him. I pray that they will help you in your life and ministry as you *"Go into all the world and preach the Gospel."* Mark 16 : 15 (MEV)

May God bless you and use you mightily for His glory.

Richard Gunning
Northern Ireland, May 2023

How to use this book...

The book contains the full transcript of six of Richard Gunning's most popular, and most used, evangelistic sermons. As you read each sermon you will notice how Richard sets the scene and gradually leads people to a point of decision about Jesus. Finally he makes a clear appeal and asks for decisions for Jesus Christ. You can use Richard's sermons in your own meetings if you want to.

After each sermon Richard gives you outlines for that sermon, very similar to the handwritten notes he would have inside his Bible as he preaches. You can use these outlines if you start to use these sermons. Or they may be helpful as a guide as to how to prepare an outline of your own sermons.

In chapters 7 and 8, Richard then shares two important teachings which he shares with young evangelists. The first one is about how to prepare a sermon, the second is about how to deliver your sermon. Both are very simple and practical and will be a great help to you if you are new to writing and preaching evangelistic sermons. There are also very practical chapters on how to lead altar calls, how to pray for the sick, how to work well with an interpreter, plus a Questions & Answers section.

The sermons in this book are all evangelistic, they are not aimed at Christians but at the unsaved and unreached. They are all well tried and tested and have been effective for over 32 years in leading multiple thousands to a faith in Jesus Christ.

This is not a theological book, it is a collection of proven sermons to help the reader in their life and ministry as an evangelist. Read each sermon, read the outline notes, and see what you can take from them. You can even give the book to unsaved friends and relatives and use it as an evangelism tool.

In the course of his evangelistic sermons Richard very rarely gives people the chapter and verse for what he is saying. The reason is that most are unsaved and have little or no knowledge at all of the Bible. He does, however, quote several verses in the course of each sermon. Scripture references are included in brackets in this book for your reference. When teaching in pastors conferences Richard then gives chapter and verse for everything he says, as most of them know the Bible well and many are taking notes.

Each sermon should take about 20 – 30 minutes to preach, without an interpreter.

May God bless you in your ministry and use you mightily as a preacher of the Gospel of Jesus Christ!

Chapter 1

"The Way to God"

In a small town in southern India, called Nandyal, an estimated crowd of well over 10,000 people have gathered under an evening sky on a local field. People sit on a huge "sea" of colourful carpets. Local choirs, singers and musicians have been leading worship and singing for at least two hours. Now the scene is set for the preaching of the Gospel. Evangelist Richard Gunning, a former hotel barman from Belfast, Northern Ireland, comes forward with his interpreter and takes the microphone.

I want to speak to you tonight about the way to God. For many years now I have travelled to many different countries. There are many differences between various countries that I have visited. They have different food, different languages, different cultures, and different religions. But one thing is always the same. No matter where I go people are looking for God. There is something in the heart of every man and every woman, every boy, and every girl, that wants to find God and make contact with God and have a relationship with Him. But why does it seem so hard to find God? Is God hiding Himself from us? No! God loves us and wants to have a relationship with us. But to come close to God we must find the way to God, and God has given us a book which tells us how to find Him, and know Him, and have a wonderful relationship with Him.

God's instruction book

In my hand I have a copy of the Bible. The Bible is a wonderful book and I believe it is the word of God. It's a history book, because it tells us how life began and how God created the heavens and the earth. How he created the first man and the first woman, and everything we see all around us. The Bible is also a prophetic book. It tells us about what will happen in the future. It tells how this world age will end and how Jesus Christ will return to earth as the ruler of the world. But the Bible is also an instruction book, written by the God who made you and me. In the same way, if you buy a radio, a motorbike, or a mobile phone, you get an instruction book. That book has been written by the people who made that thing. They give you an instruction book so that you can operate that thing correctly, they want you to be happy and to enjoy the thing they have made and which you have now bought. That is why it is important to read the instruction book whenever one is included with anything you buy.

The Foolish Man

Many times people do not bother to read the instruction book. Either they are too lazy to read it, or they think they are very clever and can work it out for themselves. I heard a story once about a very foolish man who bought a radio in a local shop. He opened the box and immediately saw the instruction book, but he tossed it to one side. You see he thought he was a clever guy, so he didn't need to read the instructions. He decided that the radio was a little dusty, so he got a bucket of water and submerged his new radio in a bucket of soap and water. He left it in the sun to dry before he tried to turn it on. Sometime later he decided to listen to the evening news on his nice clean radio. But of course it didn't work! It just made a terrible noise and then there was silence. He picked up the instruction book and put the radio back in the box and went back to the shop. "This radio doesn't work!" he shouted angrily at the shop keeper. "Well it was fine when you bought it," said the shopkeeper. "What did you do to it when you got home?" The foolish man explained that he had washed the radio in a bucket of soap and water. The shopkeeper laughed and asked the foolish man if he had read the instruction book before using the radio? Of course he had to say that he had not even looked at the instruction book. "Well" said the shopkeeper, "it says clearly on page one, "Do not allow the radio to get wet as this will destroy it!". You see the foolish man got a lot of trouble with his radio because he did not read the instruction book.

God who created you and me has given us an instruction book, we call it the Bible. It is quite a big book, it contains many chapters and verses. I don't have time tonight to preach the whole Bible to you. But I want tonight to read one verse to you, and it is a very important verse which sums up the main message the Bible wants to tell us. In John Chapter 14 and verse 6 (NKJV) Jesus Christ, the Son of God, God revealed in the flesh, said these words: *I am the way, the truth, and the life. No one comes to the Father except through me.* That is a very powerful statement for anyone to make. Jesus tells us, in this instruction book, that He is the way to God. In fact He says He is the **only** way to God!

The way to God

Some people say, "all religions lead to God," but that is not correct. I came to this town yesterday in a car. My driver had to be very careful to find the right road that would bring us safely to this place. If he had taken the wrong road, we would have ended up somewhere else and not here. It was important that we chose the right road, the road that would bring us to this town. In the same way, if we want to find God, and know God, and spend eternity with Him in Heaven, then we must find the way that leads to God. It would be foolish to say that all roads lead to this place. We all know that that is not correct, many roads lead to other places. To get to where we want to go in life, we must find the right road. It is the same spiritually speaking, to find God and reach Heaven after we die, it is vital that we choose the right road.

Why is Jesus the only way?

"But why is Jesus the only way?" people ask. Let me try to answer that question as simply as I can. You see in the beginning God created the heavens and the earth and everything we see all around us. Then He created the first man and the first woman. The Bible tells us that when God had finished creating everything that it was good. God created a perfect and sin free world. There was no war or fighting or hatred. There was no sickness or disease, no hunger, or tears. Everything was beautiful and perfect when God created the world in the beginning. But then something terrible happened, the devil came into this world. When he was created, he was a beautiful and high-ranking angel, but he rebelled against God and was thrown out of heaven. One third of the angels also followed him and they are what we call demons today.

The devil is totally wicked and evil. He hates God and everything God has created. The Bible tells us that his only desire is to *"to steal and to kill and to destroy."* (John 10 : 10 NKJV)

You see the devil is the total opposite of God. God is good and the devil is bad. God wants to bless you, but the devil wants to destroy you. God wants you to spend eternity in heaven with him, but the devil wants you to be with him in the fires of hell. Please lift your hand and wave it at me if you are listening, because this is very important for you and your soul, and where you will spend eternity.

Separated from God

The devil decided to try and lead the first man and the first woman away from God. Sadly, they listened to the lies the devil told them and they turned their backs on God and started to follow after the devil. At that moment, it was as if a big wall came down which separated the first man and the first woman from God. They were now on one side with the devil, and God was on the other side of this spiritual wall. God and all His blessings were on one side, but the man and woman were now stuck with the devil and his demons. There was no way back to God. Now all the bad things started to happen. Sickness and disease came, wars and fighting came. All the bad things we see all around us in this world started to happen, because the man and the woman made a terrible choice and started to follow the devil.

Good News!

This is not good news so far this evening. But I have good news for you tonight! God did not leave us alone. God did not abandon us to the devil and his demons. God decided to make a plan that would save us from the devil and his demons. God made a plan to save us all, if we will only believe and follow

His plan. God decided to send His Son, Jesus Christ, into the world to save men and women from their sin and from all the works of the devil. Jesus Christ, who is God in human form, came to earth over 2,000 years ago. He was born as a little baby in a town called Bethlehem in the nation we call Israel today. He grew up in a town called Nazareth, but the Bible does not tell us much about his childhood years. But one thing we do know about Jesus is that he never sinned. That is the difference between us and Jesus, the Bible says that He was tempted in every way, just like you and me, but He never sinned. Jesus came to show us what God is like. He said, *"He who has seen me has seen the Father."* (John 14 : 9 MEV) In another verse He said, *"My Father and I are one."* (John 10 : 30 MEV)

What kind of God does Jesus Christ reveal to us? The Bible tells us that, *"He went about doing good."* (Acts 10 : 38 NKJV) Jesus went around doing good things. He forgave people their sins. He healed the sick, He fed the hungry. Sometimes He even raised people from the dead, like his friend Lazarus. Jesus shows us that God is good, and that God is love, just as the Bible says. Jesus shows us that God is the direct opposite of the devil whose only purpose is *"to steal and to kill and to destroy."* (John 10 : 10 NKJV)

Jesus went about on earth doing all these good things. He preached to huge crowds of people and many of them started to tun their back on the devil and follow Jesus Christ. Of course the devil wasn't happy about this at all. He was losing followers every day, because people had now realised that Jesus is the way back to God, for whoever will believe in Him.

The devil's evil plan

The devil didn't like what was happening. Now people were leaving him and flocking to Jesus Christ. People did not want to stay with the devil any longer, now God had provided a way out, a way back to God and that way is a person, Jesus Christ, the Son of the living God. That's why Jesus said *"I am the way, the truth, and the life. No one comes to the Father except through me."* (John 14 : 6 NKJV)

The devil decided that he must devise a plan to get rid of Jesus. He thought that if he did that, then everything would be ok, and people would be unable to leave him and return back to God. The devil came into the hearts of some evil men, and they came one night and arrested Jesus. Then they accused him falsely of many different things. Finally Jesus was sentenced to death, by being nailed to a cross made of wood. Jesus suffered a terrible beating and then he was taken outside the city and nailed to a cross. Then the cross was lifted up and Jesus was left there to die, with two criminals beside Him. He hung there in terrible pain, with nails in his hands and nails in His feet. There on that cross over 2,000 years ago Jesus Christ died for the sins of us all.

But why did God allow His Son to die? Why did God not stop these evil men and save His Son? The answer to that question is very simple. When Jesus died on the cross, He was not suffering because of His own sins, because the Bible tells us He was without sin. No, he was dying for your sin and for my sin, and for the sins of everyone in the world. You see He took your place, He took my place. He took the place of everyone who has ever lived and everyone who will live in the future.

The condemned man

Let me explain it in another way, to help you understand. Imagine you had committed a terrible crime and the police came and arrested you. You are brought to the court and the judge carefully considers your case and listens to all the evidence. However, you know that you are guilty, and that you deserve to be punished. Eventually the judge says that you are guilty and starts to announce the punishment you will receive.

"This crime is so serious" he says, "I sentence you to death!" Then the police take you back to prison and you are placed in the condemned prisoner's cell to await the day of your execution. The day and the hour arrive, and the time has come for you to be executed. Suddenly you hear footsteps in the corridor outside your cell. The guards are on their way to take you to the place of execution, in a few minutes time you will be dead. Now your heart is beating quickly, now you are afraid. What will happen to you after you die? The door to your cell opens and the governor of the prison comes in, he has a smile on his face. "My friend" he says, "I have good news for you!" You are shocked by this announcement. "What is the good news?" you ask. "I thought you had come to take me outside and execute me?" But the governor replies" Oh no, you see a good man came one hour ago. He told us that he loved you so much that he wanted to die in your place. So a short time ago we executed him instead of you, you are free to go home. The punishment for your crime has been paid because someone took your place." You would be overcome with joy and with thankfulness that someone was willing to die in your place, someone was willing to take your punishment. Someone loved you enough to do that for you!

2,000 years ago that is exactly what Jesus Christ did for you and for me, and for everyone who will believe. You see God is a holy God and God must punish sin, and the Bible tells us that the punishment, or wages, for sin is death. But God loved us all so much that He sent His only Son, that whoever believes in Him should not perish but have everlasting life. Jesus Christ took your place, He took my place and the place of everyone here tonight. All we have to do is to believe it and to thank Him for dying in our place. Your sins are forgiven by faith in Jesus and His death on the cross, not by keeping a lot of religious rules and regulations. There is only one person who died for the sins of the world, only one person who took the punishment for our sins, only one person who can save us from sin and from the devil, and only one person who is the way back to God – that person is Jesus Christ.

Risen from the dead

For a short time the devil thought his plan had succeeded. "Now the Son of God is dead" he thought to himself. "There is no way back to God for people." But on the third day God showed that he is more powerful than the devil. God showed that He is more powerful even than death itself. On the third day God raised Jesus Christ up from the dead, hallelujah! Jesus appeared to his friends and then to many other people. He even allowed a man called Thomas to place his fingers in the holes in his hands, and to touch His side, so that he would believe that Jesus truly was alive.

Then Jesus gathered together all His friends on a hill outside Jerusalem. He told them that the time had come for Him to go back up to Heaven. But He also told them that He would not leave them alone. "In a few days' time you will all be filled with the Holy Spirit," Jesus said. "Then I want you to go into all the world and tell people that I am alive and that I am the way to God. And I will be with you, and I will confirm the message you preach by healing many sick people when you pray for them." The disciples went into the city and started to do as Jesus had commanded them.

Gradually this message of Jesus Christ, as the way back to God, began to spread to many places in the world. That is why we have come here tonight, that is why we are having these meetings. We are not here to sell you something. We are not here to make you a member of a religion. We have come to tell you that you can find the way back to God tonight. We have come to tell you that Jesus Christ is the way, the truth, and the life, and that no man or woman, no boy or girl, can come back to God unless they believe in Jesus Christ.

So what about you tonight? Have you found God, or are you still seeking? Do you know that your sins are forgiven? Do you know that you will go to Heaven when you die? What about you, and you, and you? Have you asked Jesus Christ to be your Saviour and to bring you back to God? Or are you trusting in your religion? Let me tell you that religion cannot save you. Religion is something man does, religion is the hand of man trying to reach up to God. Religion is rules and regulations and ceremonies. But the Gospel of Jesus Christ that I preach tonight is the hand of God reaching down to men and women in the person of Jesus Christ! What about you tonight? Do you have peace with God through our Lord and Saviour Jesus Christ? The Bible says, *"Everyone who calls upon the name of the Lord will be saved."* (Romans 10 : 13 NIV) What about you, have you called on the name of Jesus and asked Him to save you from sin and the devil? Or are you still walking around in spiritual darkness, hoping to someday find the way to God?

My friends, I want to tell you that as a sinful young man I asked Jesus Christ into my life. I asked Him to save me from sin and to bring me back to God. He came into my heart and made me a new person. He took away all my sin and gave me peace with God. Now I have come here tonight to share this good news with you.

Decision time

Now you must make a decision, now you must make a choice. Either you will say "yes" to Jesus Christ and receive Him as your Saviour, or you will reject Him and go home tonight still deep in sin and without hope and without God in this world. This is your opportunity to get right with God tonight, by opening your heart to Jesus Christ and asking Him to save your soul and to cleanse you from all your sins. My friends, there is no other way, no other possibility, no other Saviour. Jesus Christ is the only way.

I ask you all right now to stand to your feet and to be quiet just for a moment. Please bow your head and close your eyes. I don't want any talking, or anyone moving around. This is a holy moment in the presence of Almighty God. Now, whilst every head is bowed and every eye is closed, let me ask you this question. How many of you here tonight want to accept Jesus Christ as your Saviour and find the way back to God this evening? Please raise your hand in the air and wave it at me. *(All around the ground many hands are raised and waving under a floodlit sky.)* All over this place many hands are raised, God bless you! Now, I want you to take the next step. All of you that raised your hands, please come to this area in front of the platform and I will lead you in a prayer to ask Jesus Christ into your heart and to bring you back to God.

Hundreds of people begin to walk quickly to a vast area in front of the platform to pray the sinners' prayer, a copy of the prayer is on page 133 of this book. After leading the crowd in the sinners' prayer Richard then gives them some basic instructions: start to pray to God every day in the name of Jesus Christ, read the Gospel of John everyone has been given, and start to attend a Bible believing church. A large team of local counsellors come forward and record the contact details of everyone who has come forward, the cards will be given to local pastors who will follow up and invite people to church.

Once the counsellors have finished recording all the names Richard then prays one prayer of healing over the crowd. Details of the prayer and how to conduct this part of the meeting, which is vital, are in chapter 10 of this book. Many people come to the platform steps after the prayer and testify that Jesus Christ has healed them. The most dramatic cases are allowed onto the platform, after being checked by local pastors, and tell the crowd what Jesus has done for them.

An altar call in one of Richard Gunning's campaigns in India.

The Way to God – sermon outline

Text: John 14 : 6 (MEV)
"I am the way the truth and the life. No one comes to the Father, except through me."

Introduction:

- Different countries have different languages, food, and cultures.
- But everyone is looking for God.
- Bible is a history book, a prophetic book, but also an INSTRUCTION book.
- Story of the fool who bought a RADIO and washed it.
- John 14 : 6 tells us the way to God is a person – Jesus Christ!
- "I am the way, the truth, and the life. No one comes to the Father, except through Me."
- All religions do not lead to God. To get to this town my driver had to take the right road that leads to this place.

Why is Jesus the only way?

- Explain about creation and the sin fall of man.
- A wall comes down and man is separated from God.
- Bad things start to happen because man is with the devil.
- God's rescue plan
- God decides to save mankind and sends Jesus Christ down to earth.
- Jesus reveals a good God, who saves, heals, and meets needs.
- People leave the devil and return to God because Jesus is the way.

The devil's evil plan

- Devil did not like people leaving his side.
- Makes a plan to hit back.
- Jesus is falsely accused of many things.
- Jesus is given a terrible beating.
- Taken outside the city and nailed to a cross.
- Two criminals with him, one on each side.
- Left to die in terrible pain on the cross.
- Devil thought he had won a great victory and killed the Son of God.

Why did God allow His Son to die?

- God is a holy God, He must punish sin.
- But God loves us so much He put all our punishment on Jesus.
- Story of the CONDEMNED MAN, someone else took his place.
- 2,000 years ago Jesus Christ died for everyone, took our punishment.
- We must believe that and gratefully receive it.

Risen from the dead!

- Devil thought he had won a great victory.
- But on the third day Jesus showed He is stronger than the devil and even death.
- On the third day Jesus arose and appeared to his disciples.
- Thomas put his finger in the nail holes in His hands.

The Great Commission

- Jesus gathered all His disciples on a hill.
- Gives them His final instruction "Go into all the world and preach the Gospel!"
- Jesus promises that His Spirit will be with them.
- He promises to confirm the Gospel by healing the sick.
- Jesus said if you will believe in Him and call upon His name you will be saved from your sins and will go to a wonderful eternal life.

Decision time

- God gives everyone freewill, we are not created like machines.
- Now you need to make a decision about Jesus.
- Will you accept Him or reject Him?
- Please stand up and close your eyes and be quiet for a moment.

Altar call and prayer

Chapter 2

"The Two Kingdoms"

The town of Lodwar in Northwest Kenya is the largest town in an arid area inhabited by the Turkana tribe, an unreached people group amongst whom RTU has been preaching the Gospel since 1990. In the centre of town a wooden platform has been constructed. Many people have gathered to hear the Gospel and to receive prayer for healing. After a time of worship, Evangelist Richard Gunning, and his interpreter Pastor Peter Karangu are invited to come to the platform and speak to the people.

I want to read a short verse to you tonight from the Bible. This is the Word of God and I believe it with all my heart. The Bible speaks to every man and every woman, every boy, and every girl. It doesn't matter who you are or where you come from. It doesn't matter if you are black or white, African, or European, God's word speaks to us all. Let me read this verse from Colossians Chapter 1 and verses 13 and 14 (MEV): *"He has delivered us from the power of darkness and has transferred us into the kingdom of His Dear Son, in whom we have redemption through His Blood, the forgiveness of sins."*

Physical and spiritual kingdoms

In this physical world in which we live, there are many different countries, or kingdoms. Each country has its own president or king. Each country has its own culture and languages. Each country also has its own borders which separate it from neighbouring countries. In this physical

20

world, which is all around us tonight, there are nearly 200 different countries. Kenya is a country, Uganda is a country, USA is a country, China is a country. But all around us tonight there is also a spiritual world. We cannot see it or touch it, but it exists and is all around us and all over the world we can see. The spiritual world is where God and His angels are moving and operating. It is also the world where the devil and his evil spirits are moving. In that spiritual world there are only two kingdoms, only two possibilities.

Here this evening we are all physically speaking in Kenya. But spiritually speaking we all also live in one of the two spiritual kingdoms. Either you live in the Kingdom of God, or you live in the Kingdom of the Devil. There is no place in the middle, no middle ground. Spiritually speaking you live in one of these two kingdoms and there is no place in the middle. Maybe you didn't know that, maybe you had not understood that, but each and every one of us lives in one of the two spiritual kingdoms.

The two spiritual rulers

In every physical country in the world, the government is very important. If your country has a good government, which treats people well, then life will be better. But if a country has a bad and evil government then life can be very bad and hard. Just as every physical country has a government, the same thing is true in the two spiritual kingdoms.
The Kingdom of God is ruled by Jesus Christ, the Son of God. In the Bible Jesus is also called "The King." Jesus is the King in the Kingdom of God. The Bible tells us that Jesus Christ is a very good king. When He lived here on earth 2,000 years ago the Bible tells us that He went about doing good things. Jesus

is a good king who wants to bless everyone who lives in the Kingdom of God. He wants to forgive us for all the bad things we have done. He wants to heal the sick. The Bible says, *"He went about doing good and healing all who were oppressed by the devil."* (Acts 10 : 38 MEV) Everywhere He went He met peoples' needs. He fed the hungry, He did miracles, He even raised people from the dead! Jesus himself said, *"I came that they might have life and have it more abundantly."* (John 10 : 10 MEV) When we die, Jesus wants to bring us to Heaven to enjoy a wonderful eternal life there with Him. In Heaven there will be no more suffering, no more pain, no more sickness, no more death. The Bible says every tear will be wiped away. Heaven sounds like a wonderful place to go to, doesn't it?

The Kingdom of the Devil is ruled over by a wicked spirit called Satan. In the beginning he was a holy angel of God, one of the highest angels in Heaven. But Satan rebelled against God and wanted to take over. God could not allow this wicked rebellion in Heaven, so Satan was thrown out of Heaven, together with one third of the angels who followed him. Today we call them demons or evil spirits. Satan is the opposite of Jesus Christ. The Bible tells us that his only purpose is to steal, to kill and to destroy. All the bad things we see happening all around us are due to the influence of the devil in this world. If you feel something is happening in your life which is stealing, killing, or destroying, then the devil is behind it. Don't blame God because God is a good god. The devil is the one to blame for all the wicked and evil things we see happening all around us. When we die, the devil wants us to spend eternity with him in a terrible place which the Bible calls Hell, which is a lake of fire. The devil knows that that is where he will end up one day, but he wants to bring as many people as possible with him.

Which kingdom are you in?

So, let me ask you this very important question tonight. Which spiritual kingdom do YOU live in? Maybe you never thought about it before? Maybe you didn't know about these two spiritual kingdoms, until I told you about them. Ask yourself that question right now: Which spiritual kingdom am I living in? Let me explain to you how you can know which kingdom you live in. When Jesus came to earth, He said this *"I am the way the truth and the life, no one comes to the Father except through me."* (John 14 : 6 MEV) The Bible also tells us that, *"if you confess with your mouth Jesus is Lord, and believe in your heart that God has raised him from the dead, you will be saved!"* (Romans 10 : 9 MEV)

You see if you have never asked Jesus into your life, then spiritually speaking you live in the Kingdom of the Devil. Now I am not saying that you are a bad person or a devil worshipper, or anything like that. But spiritually speaking you are living in the devil's kingdom. Because we can only enter into the Kingdom of God by asking Jesus to come into our lives and to save us from the devil and his kingdom. Have you ever done that? Have you ever asked Jesus to come into your life, to forgive your sins and to give you eternal life?

No middle ground

Some people try to tell me: "I am not very good, but I am not very bad. I am somewhere in the middle. I am not a Christian, but I am not a bad person, spiritually I am just somewhere in the middle." Many people think like that when it comes to spiritual things. They think there is a middle ground between the two spiritual kingdoms. They think that they do not need to make a choice because they are just somewhere in the middle. But that is not true, there is no middle ground between the two spiritual kingdoms.

Let me explain this in a different way. If you travel north from here, you will eventually come to a border between Kenya and Ethiopia A border is a line which separates one country from another country. Usually you will see a fence which marks the border. You are either on one side of the border, or you are on the other side, but there is no space in the middle. Usually at the border you will meet some soldiers who are there to check people if they want to cross the border. On one side you will meet the soldiers of Kenya, and on the other side you will see the soldiers of Ethiopia.

When you approach that border then you have to make a decision. Will I stay in Kenya, or will I cross the border and enter Ethiopia? You cannot live on the border, that is not permitted. If you try to build a house on the border the soldiers will come quickly and tell you: "You are not allowed to live on the border, you must decide if you want to live in Kenya, or in Ethiopia, but you cannot live on the border!" It is the same in the spiritual world which is all around us. You must make an important decision, will you live in the Kingdom of God, or in the Kingdom of the Devil, but there is no place in the middle.

Changing kingdoms

Maybe you have realised tonight that you are living in the devil's kingdom? You know that you are in the wrong place spiritually speaking, and you want to get out of there. I have good news for you this evening, you can change sides. You can leave the Kingdom of the Devil and cross the border into the

Kingdom of God. On the outside you will still look the same. You will still live in the same country that you live in now. But in the spiritual world something amazing has happened. You have crossed the spiritual border, out of the Kingdom of Satan and into the Kingdom of God. Spiritually speaking the devil no longer has power over you. Why not? Because you no longer live in his kingdom. You have crossed the border into a new kingdom with a new king!

The President of Kenya has no power in Ethiopia, once he comes to the border his power ends. The President of America has no power in Canada, once he comes to the border his power ends. In the same way the devil has no power in the Kingdom of God, once you cross the border, he has no power over you!

Refugees are turned back

Many times we hear about refugees on the television. When life is bad in a country, or there is a lot of violence and war, many people try to move to a neighbouring country. Often they pack up their belongings and go the border of the next country. They hope that life will be better there and that they will be able to live in peace. They go to the border of the neighbouring country and ask to be allowed to cross. But many times the soldiers on the border turn them away. They sometimes say: "Sorry but we already have too many people in our country, we cannot allow you to cross the border and come in here. Go back to where you came from, we are not going to allow you to enter our country." However, in the spiritual world nobody is ever turned away at the border of the Kingdom of God. Jesus himself said, *"whoever comes to Me I will never drive away"* (John 6 : 37 NIV) Everyone is welcome in the

Kingdom of God, nobody who comes to Jesus will be rejected. The Bible tells us *"Everyone who calls on the name of the Lord shall be saved."* (Romans 10 : 13 MEV) There is no possibility of rejection, no possibility of anyone being turned away. Good or bad, rich or poor. There is room in the Kingdom of God for everyone who wishes by faith in Jesus to enter in!

The devil and his lies

Of course the devil will try to stop you if you think of leaving his kingdom, he wants you to stay with him. His main tactic is to tell you lies. You see the devil is a *"a liar and the father of lies,"* just as Jesus said. (John 8 : 44 NIV)

He will try different lies to get you to stay on his side, here are a few of them:
- "You don't need to follow Jesus and believe in Him, stay here with me and you will be fine. God will let you into Heaven when you die."
- "You don't need to go over to the Kingdom of God, just try to be a good person and things will be fine."
- "Just follow your religion, God doesn't care what you believe, as long as you are sincere."
- "Stay here with me and you can commit all the sins you like and have a great time."

He will try everything he can to encourage you to stay in his kingdom of darkness. Don't listen to the lies of the devil. Make a decision to cross the border tonight into the Kingdom of God.

How do I change kingdoms?

In the Gospel of John Chapter 3, Jesus met a very religious man called Nicodemus. This man was a religious teacher. He knew a lot about God, and he knew a lot about religion, but spiritually speaking he still lived in the Kingdom of the Devil. You see religion cannot save you and bring you into the Kingdom of God. Religion is something man does. Religion is rules and ceremonies and regulations. Religion is the hand of man trying to reach up and touch God, but it never works. The Gospel of Jesus Christ, however, is the hand of God reaching down to men and women and rescuing anyone who asks to be saved from the devil's kingdom.

That man Nicodemus had many questions. He knew that Jesus was different. He knew that Jesus was the Son of God and the Saviour of the world, but still he was confused. He wondered about the Kingdom of God and how to enter it. Jesus looked at him and said: *"Unless a man is born again, he cannot see the kingdom of God."* (John 3 : 5 MEV) Now Nicodemus was very confused, because he was thinking about physical birth, not spiritual birth. Nicodemus asked Jesus how can anyone go back into his mother's womb and be born again? But Jesus was talking about a spiritual rebirth, not a physical rebirth. You see when you call upon the name of Jesus and ask Him to save you and bring you into the Kingdom of God, then on the inside you are born again. The Bible says: *"If any man is in Christ, he is a new creature. Old things have passed away. Look, all things have become new."* (1st Corinthians 5 : 17 MEV) Physically speaking we cannot be born again, but spiritually speaking it is possible and it is essential if we want to enter the Kingdom of God.

The A, B, C of the Gospel

How can we be born again spiritually and enter the kingdom of God? How do we cross the spiritual border, out of the Kingdom of Satan and into the Kingdom of God? The answer is very simple, there are three things you need to do:

Admit – admit that you have sinned and done wrong in the eyes of a holy God.

Believe, believe that Jesus Christ is the Son of God who came in the flesh and died on the cross to take the punishment for your sin and my sin. Believe that He rose again from the dead on the third day. The Bible says: *"If you confess with your mouth Jesus is Lord and believe in your heart that God has raised Him from the dead, you will be saved."* (Romans 10 : 13 MEV)

Confess which simply means to say out loud that Jesus Christ is now your Saviour and your Lord. When you confess that Jesus is Lord, you are recognising Him as your King. He immediately launches a rescue operation in the spiritual world. He lifts you up out of the Kingdom of Satan, across the border and He places you in the Kingdom of God. Now the devil has no power over you because you no longer live in his kingdom. You have crossed the border spiritually speaking, you have a new citizenship, a new King. You are a new person, the old things have passed away. Now you are right with God, cleansed from sin and a citizen of the Kingdom of God. The devil might still try and shout at you in your head from his side of the border. He might try and tell you to come back to his side. He might try to tell you that he still has power over you, don't listen to his lies. The Bible says: *"Submit yourselves to God. Resist the devil, and he will flee from you."* (James 4 : 7 MEV)

28

(Note: If you are preaching in English and without an interpreter, you can talk about the "A, B, C of the Gospel." Tell people to be saved is as simple as A, B, C. But this will not work well if you are using an interpreter into a different language. Then you can just tell them to admit, believe and confess.)

Changing kingdoms is not a matter of doing many good works or keeping many religious rules and regulations. No, salvation is by simple faith in Jesus Christ and by calling on His name and asking Him to save you and forgive you. He will never refuse you, He will never turn you away. It doesn't matter how bad you are, He is willing to save you. It doesn't matter how good and nice you think you are, you still need Jesus to save you. It doesn't matter how religious you are, because religion cannot save you.

My story

I grew up in a Christian family. I went to church every Sunday with my parents. But I was far away from God. I did not know Jesus Christ, I was not a citizen of His kingdom. Spiritually speaking I lived in the devil's kingdom. But then one day I heard this message I have been speaking to you about this evening. I prayed a simple prayer and asked Jesus Christ to come into my heart and to forgive me for all my sins. When I finished my prayer, I still lived in the same house and in the same country. But I soon realised that something had changed, my life was different. You see I had been lifted out of the Kingdom of Satan and into the Kingdom of God. Jesus was now my Saviour and my King. I had been "born again" just as Jesus had said to Nicodemus the religious leader.

The challenge

So my friends here tonight, I have a question for you. Which spiritual kingdom are you living in? Do you live in the devil's kingdom, or do live in the Kingdom of God? There are only two possibilities, there is no place in the middle, either you are on one side or the other side. If you have never asked Jesus Christ to save you then spiritually speaking, you are still in the devil's kingdom. I am not saying that you are a devil worshipper or anything like that. But spiritually you do not live in the Kingdom of God where we all should be. You might be a good person and try to live a good life, but spiritually the devil has power over you because you live in his kingdom. But tonight you can change sides! Tonight you can cross the spiritual border, out of the devil's kingdom and into the Kingdom of God. You see you have a choice tonight, God has given us all freewill. God will never force anyone to live in His Kingdom, He gives you a free choice.

Right now I am going to ask you to make a decision. Please stand to your feet, close your eyes, and bow your head. Let's all be quiet for a minute in the presence of Almighty God. I don't want anyone to be talking or moving around, this is a very serious moment in your life tonight. So, whilst every head is bowed and every eye closed, let me ask this question tonight. How many of you want to cross the spiritual border tonight? How many of you want to leave the devil's kingdom and cross the border into the Kingdom of God? How many of you want Jesus Christ to come and save you, and lift you over the border into His good kingdom? How many of you want that tonight? Please lift your hand right now and wave it at me! (All around the ground many hands are raised and waving under the African sky.) All over this place many hands are raised, God bless you. Now I want you to take the next step. All of you that raised your hands, please come to this area in front of the platform, and I will lead you in a prayer to ask Jesus Christ to come and save you out of the devil's kingdom and bring you into the Kingdom of God.

Hundreds of people begin to walk quickly to a vast area in front of the platform to pray the sinners' prayer, a copy of the prayer is on page 133 of this book. After leading the crowd in the sinners' prayer Richard then gives them some basic instructions: start to pray to God every day in the name of Jesus Christ and start to attend a Bible believing church. A large team of local counsellors come forward and record the contact details of everyone who has come forward, the cards will be given to local pastors who will follow up and invite people to church.

Once the counsellors have finished recording all the names Richard then prays one prayer of healing over the crowd. Details of the prayer and how to conduct this part of the meeting, which is vital, are on page 133 of this book. Many people come to the platform steps after the prayer and testify that Jesus Christ has healed them. The most dramatic cases are allowed onto the platform, after being checked by local pastors, and tell the crowd what Jesus has done for them.

Altar call in Burkina Faso, West Africa.

The Two Kingdoms – sermon outline

Text: Colossians 1 : 13 – 14 (MEV)
"He has delivered us from the power of darkness and has transferred us into the kingdom of His dear Son, in whom we have redemption through His blood, the forgiveness of sins."

Introduction:

- Nearly 200 countries in his physical world, e.g. China, USA, Kenya.
- Only two countries or kingdoms in the spiritual world.
- Governments affect our lives, for good or evil.
- Kingdom of God ruled by Jesus, Kingdom of Satan ruled by the devil.
- Describe the differences between Jesus and the devil.
- John 10 : 10 (MEV) "The thief does not come, except to steal and kill and destroy. I came that they may have life and that they may have it more abundantly."
- Which spiritual kingdom are you living in?

No Middle Ground

- No middle ground between the two spiritual kingdoms.
- Example of a land border between two countries.
- You have to make a choice, stay, or move across the border.

Changing kingdoms

- Good news tonight! You can change kingdoms.
- Devil will have no power over you.

- President of China has no power in Russia, power ends at the border.

Refugees

- People who want to leave a troubled country and move to another one.
- Often turned back at the border.
- Jesus will never turn anyone away.
- Devil will tell you lies to get you to stay in his kingdom.

How to change spiritual kingdoms

- Jesus and Nicodemus, "You must be born again."
- "Unless a man is born again, he cannot see the kingdom of God." (John 3:5)
- When you accept Jesus you become a "new creature."
- 2 Corinthians 5 : 17: "If any man is in Christ, he is a new creature. Look, all things have become new."
- The A, B, C of the Gospel. ADMIT, BELIEVE, CONFESS.
- Romans 10 : 13 (MEV)"If you confess with your mouth Jesus is Lord and believe in your heart that God has raised Him from the dead, you will be saved."

Share your testimony

- Briefly share your own testimony. How you "changed kingdoms."

Decision time

- Now you must make a decision.
- Which spiritual kingdom do you choose to live in?
- God gives you a choice tonight. Only you can decide.
- But tonight you can leave the Kingdom of the devil and move into the Kingdom of God.
- If you call on the name of Jesus you will be saved, rescued, delivered out of the devil's kingdom. Romans 10 : 13 (MEV) "Everyone who calls on the name of the Lord shall be saved."
- Jesus will bring you across the border and place you in the Kingdom of God for this life and for eternity.

Altar call and prayer

Chapter 3

Standing by the Cross

(This sermon is based on a message originally preached by Richard's mentor and "spiritual father" the late Dr Aril Edvardsen, 1938 – 2008, from Norway.)

Under an African sky in the West African nation of Burkina Faso, thousands of people have gathered on a dusty football pitch in a small town called Reo. They have come to a "Festival of Good News." Posters have been put up all around the town, and thousands of handbills have been distributed. The meetings have also been widely announced on local radio. A variety of church choirs and singers have been leading worship for over two hours. RTU Ministries' local campaign director now invites Evangelist Richard Gunning and his interpreter to come and share the word of God.

Different attitudes

It's a great joy to be with you this evening and to have this opportunity to share good news with you. You see the Gospel of Jesus Christ is good news, the word "gospel" means good news and that is why we have come to your town to have this festival. We want to share good news with you this evening.

Tonight I want to speak to you about the most dramatic and important event in the history of the world. This event happened over 2,000 years ago, but it is just as relevant and important today as it was over 2,000 years ago. I want to talk to you tonight about the death of Jesus Christ on the cross. The Bible tells us in John Chapter 19 verses 17 – 26 (NKJV) about the death of Jesus Christ. It also tells us about different people who were involved in his death, or who were standing close by and watching everything that was happening on that great and terrible day. These people who were all close to the execution of Jesus Christ all had different attitudes to Jesus. Even though these events happened over 2,000 years ago, we still find those same attitudes represented in different people today. Let us all listen carefully to what the Bible says about this great and terrible day in John Chapter 19 verses 17 - 30:

"And He, bearing His cross, went out to a place called the Place of a Skull, which is called in Hebrew, Golgotha,[8] *where they crucified Him, and two others with Him, one on either side, and Jesus in the centre. Now Pilate wrote a title and put it on the cross. And the writing was: JESUS OF NAZARETH, THE KING OF THE JEWS. Then many of the Jews read this title, for the place where Jesus was crucified was near the city; and it was written in Hebrew, Greek, and Latin. Therefore the chief priests of the Jews said to Pilate, "Do not write, 'The King of the Jews,' but, He said, "I am the King of the Jews." Pilate answered, "What I have written, I have written." Then the soldiers, when they had crucified Jesus, took His garments and made four parts, to each soldier a part, and also the tunic. Now the tunic was without seam, woven from the top in one piece. They said therefore among themselves, "Let us not tear it, but cast lots for it, whose it shall be," that the Scripture might be fulfilled which says: "They divided My garments among them, and for My clothing they cast lots. "Therefore the soldiers did these things. Now there stood by the cross of Jesus His mother, and His mother's sister, Mary the wife of Clopas, and Mary Magdalene*[6] *When Jesus therefore saw His mother, and the disciple whom He loved standing by, He said to His mother, "Woman, behold your son!"*[7] *Then He said to the disciple, "Behold your mother!" And from that hour that disciple took her to his own home. After this, Jesus, knowing that all things were now accomplished, that the Scripture might be fulfilled, said, "I thirst!" Now a vessel full of sour wine was sitting there, and they*

filled a sponge with sour wine, put it on hyssop, and put it to his mouth. So when Jesus had received the sour wine, He said, "It is finished!" And bowing His head, He gave up His spirit."

There are many people here tonight in this meeting. And there are many different attitudes to Jesus Christ here tonight. Those same attitudes can be seen in the hearts of the people who were standing nearby, as Jesus Christ died on a cross for our sins on a hill outside Jerusalem in Israel. Tonight I want to look more closely at these different people and their different attitudes to Jesus on the cross. I believe tonight that many of you will find that your attitude is also represented by one of these people I will talk about tonight.

Pontius Pilate

The Bible tells us that standing close to the cross of Jesus Christ was a man called Pontius Pilate. Pilate was the Roman Governor of that region at that time. The Bible tells us that the Jewish religious leaders brought Jesus to Pilate because they wanted him to sentence Jesus to death. Only Pilate had the power to sentence a man to death, the religious leaders needed Pilate to pass the death sentence on Jesus. Pilate was at first reluctant to do as they asked. He spoke to Jesus, and he considered the case. He tried to question Jesus, but Jesus refused to say much to him. Pilate listened to the accusations the religious leaders were making about Jesus, but Pilate could not see that He had done anything wrong. Then his wife came to him and told Pilate that she had had a dream about Jesus, and she said: *"Don't have anything to do with that innocent man."* (Matthew 27 : 19 NIV)

Pilate listened to all the different people who were speaking to him. He listened to the religious leaders, he listened to his wife, he also listened to the large crowd that had now gathered and were waiting for his decision. As Pilate was thinking about what to do, the crowd in front of him began to chant with one voice, just like a football crowd: "Crucify him, crucify him!" Fear came into the heart of Pontius Pilate. He tried to argue with the crowd. The Bible tells us that three times Pilate said to them: "I find no fault in this man." You see Jesus is the only person who ever lived a totally sinless life. He was tempted just like you and me, but He never sinned. You can find fault in Christians you may know, you can find fault in pastors and preachers. But you will never find fault with Jesus Christ.

Then Pilate had an idea. It was customary at that time of year to release one prisoner, chosen by the people, and let him go free. Pilate knew that in the prison they had a terrible man called Barabbas, this man was a robber and a murderer, today we would probably call him a terrorist. Pilate told his soldiers to go and fetch Barabbas immediately. A short time later the soldiers returned with Barabbas, this wicked man who was guilty of terrible crimes and who had been sentenced to death. Pilate decided that the best solution would be to let the people choose between Jesus Christ and Barabbas, the terrorist leader. Surely the people would ask for Jesus to be set free, that would solve the problem. But to Pilate's horror the people began to shout: "We want Barabbas! We want Barabbas!" Fear came into the heart of Pilate, and he decided to release Barabbas and hand Jesus over to his soldiers to be crucified.

Pontius Pilate was what we call a "convinced coward." Deep in his heart he knew that Jesus was the Son of God. He could find no fault in Jesus whatsoever. But like many people today he was afraid to take a stand with Jesus. He was afraid of the crowd, afraid of the religious leaders, afraid of what people would say about him. Maybe you are here tonight, and you know that Jesus is alive and that He is the Son of God who died for your sins. Deep in your heart you know that the Gospel is true, and that Jesus is the only way to God. Deep in your heart you know that you need to accept Jesus as your Lord and Saviour. You know that spiritually speaking you need to come close to the cross of Jesus Christ by simple faith. Deep in your heart you know that you need to put your faith in Him and in His death on that terrible cross. But you are afraid of what people might say. You are afraid of your friends, your family, your neighbours. You are convinced, but you are also a coward! Don't be like Pontius Pilate tonight. When we come to the end of this meeting, we will ask people to come by faith to the cross. I urge you to be bold. I urge you to throw away your fears and to come to the cross and let the blood of Jesus Christ cleanse you from all unrighteousness this evening. Don't be like Pontius Pilate, the convinced coward.

The Religious People

Another group of people who were there were the religious leaders and their followers. In this world today there are many different religions. Many millions of people are very religious, and many of their religions teach some good things. The religious leaders, at the time Jesus was on earth, were very strict and devoted to their religion. They didn't like Jesus because he said He was the Son of God. He also boldly declared *"I am the way, the truth, and the life. No one comes to the Father, except through Me."* (John 14 : 6 MEV) They thought that their religion could save them and bring them to Heaven. But let me tell you tonight that religion cannot save you from your sins. Religion cannot give you peace with God, religion cannot bring you to Heaven.

You see religion is something man does. Religion is rules and regulations, ceremonies, and many other things. Nobody can possibly do all the things they are supposed to do. Religion is the hand of man reaching up and trying to touch God. But the Gospel of Jesus Christ, which I am preaching to you tonight, is the hand of God reaching down to men and women in the person of Jesus Christ.

These religious people had heard Jesus preaching and teaching. They had seen Him doing wonderful miracles, healing the sick, casting out demons, and turning water into wine. They had even seen the dead raised. But these religious people were so proud, and so stubborn, that they refused to come to Jesus by faith and receive forgiveness of sins. They refused to accept that their religion could not save them. They refused, by faith, to come close to the cross of Jesus Christ. Instead they mocked Jesus as He suffered on that cross. *"He saved others, Himself he cannot save."* they shouted. *"Let him now come down from the cross and we will believe Him."* (Matthew 27 : 42 NKJV)

Are you here tonight and you are like those religious people? You are trusting in your religion to save you and to bring you to Heaven when you die? But if religion was able to save us then there was no need for God to send His only Son to die for us. Don't trust in your religion tonight my friends. Only Jesus can save you from sin. Only Jesus can take you to Heaven when you die. The Bible says: *"There is no other name under Heaven given amongst men by which we must be saved."* (Acts 4 : 12 MEV)

The Soldiers

There was a third group of people also present at the death of Jesus Christ on the cross. They were the soldiers who had the terrible job of nailing Jesus, and two other men, to the three crosses made of wood. To them this was all just part of their daily work. They had done this many times before, they simply carried out the orders they were given. It didn't matter how much a man would scream or beg for mercy, they had a job to do, and they were there to do as they had been commanded. Before they nailed a prisoner to the cross the Roman soldiers took off his clothes. After the prisoner had been nailed to the cross and raised up high, they would then divide the prisoner's clothes amongst themselves and later sell them, to earn some money. Jesus had a nice robe, and they did not want to tear it, so they gambled for His clothes to see who would have them.

The thing I want to tell you about the soldiers is this. They were not interested in Jesus Christ on the cross, dying for the sins of all the world, including the sins of those Roman soldiers. No, they were interested in the things that **belonged** to Jesus, but not in Jesus Himself. There are many people like that today. Perhaps there are people like that here in this meeting this evening? You are not interested in Jesus Christ and His death for you 2,000 years ago. But you are interested in things that BELONG to Jesus. You want His blessings, you want His help, you want His healing, you want Him to answer your prayers and give you things you want. But you are not interested in accepting Jesus as the Lord and Saviour of your life. You have never come by faith to the cross of Jesus Christ and asked Him to cleanse you from all your sins. No, you are just like the Roman soldiers, only interested in the things that belong to Jesus. Don't be like the soldiers tonight. But come by faith to the cross and look up to Jesus on the cross, loving you, dying for you, taking the punishment for all your sins on that terrible cross.

The Passers By

There was another group of people who were also close to the scene when Jesus Christ was crucified 2,000 years ago. The Bible tells us the place where Jesus was crucified was close to the city of Jerusalem. Many people were passing by, close to this place of execution. I can imagine two men walking past on their way home after working in the fields. Suddenly they look up towards the hill of Golgotha and see that something is happening up there. Then they see that three crosses have been raised up, each with a man nailed firmly to his cross. They pause for a moment to look at the scene, feelings of horror and sympathy go through their minds as the sheer brutality of the scene hits them. As they look at this unfolding scene up on the hill, the first man says to his friend: "The man on the middle cross, isn't that the miracle worker, Jesus of Nazareth?" His friend takes another look and replies: "Yes, you are right, that is Him. I was in some of His meetings, He said some very interesting things. I even saw Him healing a lot of people in those meetings. That is terrible what they are doing to Him now."

The men stand watching from a distance for a few minutes as Jesus and the two thieves hang in agony on their crosses. But after a few minutes the two men who are watching decide to leave the scene. "Probably best to head home now," says one of them. "My wife will have my dinner ready, and I don't want to be late getting home." So they pass on and continue their journey home. They don't come close to the cross of Jesus Christ where we all should be, spiritually speaking.

Many people here tonight are like those two men. You have respect for Jesus Christ. You are not against Him. But you have never come by faith to the foot of the cross, spiritually speaking, and asked Jesus to cleanse you from all your sins. You are just passing by, just like those two men. You have come here tonight, and you have listened to the Gospel of Jesus Christ, you like the message. But what will you do when we close the meeting this evening, and ask people to come by faith to the cross of Jesus Christ and receive forgiveness of sins? Will you quickly leave the meeting and hurry home? Or will you come forward in faith and ask Jesus Christ to forgive you all your sins and put your faith in the fact that He took all your punishment on the cross? The Bible says, *"The wages of sin is death, but the gift of God is eternal life through Jesus Christ our Lord."* (Romans 6 : 23, MEV) Don't be like those two men this evening. Don't listen to the Gospel, but then hurry home without coming by faith to the cross of Jesus Christ and receiving forgiveness for all your sins.

The Women at the Cross

Finally, we read about another group of people who are at the scene as Jesus Christ hangs on the cross, dying for your sins and my sins, and the sins of all the world. We read that some women were also there. But there is something different about these women, the Bible tells us that they are "standing by the cross" where we all should be, spiritually speaking. These women are not passing by, they are not mocking Jesus, they are not interested in having His clothes to sell in the marketplace. No! These ordinary women are standing by the cross of Jesus, looking to Him, trusting in Him, loving Him

43

with all their hearts. They have come close to the cross of Jesus Christ, they are not afraid of what someone else may say or think about them. No! They are in the right place, the place where we all should be, spiritually speaking, standing by the cross.

The Good Person

Let us take a look at two of these women who are standing by the cross of Jesus Christ. The first lady who is standing there is Mary the mother of Jesus. She represents all the good people in the world. She had been chosen by God to be the mother of Jesus Christ. She was a good lady, a lady who was dedicated to God and who had lived a very pure and godly life. However, she still needed to come to the cross and receive forgiveness of sins. You see no matter how good you think you are, you cannot save yourself. The Bible tells us that we have all sinned and fall short of God's standards. No matter how good you think you are, you can never come up to God's standards, you can never live a perfect life. You can never live a life without sin. You might be a good person who does many good things. Perhaps you are kind to your neighbours. Perhaps you help the poor, perhaps you are very religious. Perhaps you feel that you are a very good and holy person. Perhaps you feel that you don't need to come to the cross of Jesus Christ. You are trusting in your own good deeds, in your own self-righteousness, in your religion. You think that you are so good and so holy that you don't need to come to the cross of Jesus Christ. But let me tell you tonight, if Mary needed to come to the cross then you also need to come to the cross, because nobody has lived a life without sinning.

Deep down in your heart you know that you have sinned. You know that you have done things that are wrong. You know that you need forgiveness for those bad things that you have done. Other people think that you are a very good person, but no matter how good you are, you still need to come to the cross of Jesus Christ. Mary represents people just like that, she represents all the good people in the world. There are many good people in the world today. I'm sure there are many good people here tonight. You've never done anything very bad. You try to live a good life, you try to please God, perhaps you go regularly to church, and all those things are good. But at the end of the day, you need to come by faith to the cross of Jesus Christ and receive forgiveness for your sins.

The Bad Person

A second lady who was standing at the cross, with Mary the mother of Jesus, was a lady called Mary Magdalene. She represents people who have fallen deep in sin. When she first met Jesus Christ, He cast seven demons out of her. Clearly, she had not lived a good life because seven demons had entered into her. Then one day she met Jesus Christ. He looked at her with great love in His heart. He did not love her sins and He hated the demons that had entered into her and were tormenting her. This was not His plan and will for her life, so Jesus cast the demons out of her and set her free. From that day Mary Magdalene decided to follow Jesus Christ. She believed in Him, and she wanted to serve him. Mary Magdalene represents people who have fallen deep in sin, but she came boldly to the foot of the cross.

Maybe you are here tonight, and you know that you have committed many sins. Maybe you are wondering, can God possibly save me? Can God forgive me all the terrible things I have done? Maybe you are here tonight, and you are a thief. Maybe you are here tonight, and you are an alcoholic, or a prostitute. Maybe you have committed some other terrible sin. I want to tell you tonight that there is forgiveness for you at the cross of Jesus Christ. You just need to come as you are, come with all your burdens and your sins and Jesus will forgive you. Jesus will never turn anyone away. He said *"Whoever comes to me I will never drive away."* (John 6 : 37 NIV) So come just as you are to the cross tonight, and as you come to Jesus tonight, He will cleanse you from all your sins. You can be free tonight of that terrible burden of sin you have been carrying, because Jesus took your punishment on the cross. He loves you and He died for you. He says, *"Come to me all of you who are weary and burdened and I will give you rest."* (Matthew 11 : 28 NIV) Are you carrying a heavy burden of sin tonight? Come to Jesus, come to the cross and He will give you rest, He will give you peace with God. Whether you are good, or whether you are bad. Be like the two ladies who came and stood by the cross of Jesus Christ, spiritually speaking that is the place where we all should be.

Decision Time

Now the time has come for you to make a decision. What is your attitude to Jesus Christ and His cross? Are you like Pontius Pilate, convinced that Jesus is Lord, but afraid to come to the cross and identify yourself with Him? Perhaps you are like the religious people, trusting in your religion to save you, but not in Jesus Christ who is the only way to God. The Bible says: *"there is no other name under heaven given to mankind by which we must be saved."* (Acts 4 : 12 NIV) Perhaps you are like the Roman soldiers? Only interested in the things that belong to

46

Jesus, but not interested in Jesus Himself. Or perhaps you are like the two ordinary men, just passing by? You are sympathetic to Jesus on the cross. You are not against Him, but you have never come to the cross, spiritually speaking, and asked Jesus to take away your sins and give you eternal life. You need to follow the example of the two ladies who came and stood by the cross of Jesus Christ. One of them was a good and a holy person, the other had had a very bad life before she met Jesus. Those two ladies made the right decision, they came and stood by the cross.

I ask you all to stand to your feet tonight. Let us all be quiet and bow our heads in the presence of Almighty God. Now let me ask this very important question. How many of you here tonight want to come by faith to the cross of Jesus Christ, and receive forgiveness for all your sins? How many of you want to do that tonight, let me see your hand? Lift your hand and wave it at me right now if you want to come by faith to the cross of Jesus Christ tonight! Oh, so many hands. All of you who raised your hands please come quickly to the front and I will lead you in a prayer to ask Jesus into your heart. Come forward right now!

Hundreds of people raise their hands in the air, and then begin to walk quickly to a vast area in front of the platform to pray the sinners' prayer, a copy of the prayer is on page 133 of this book. After leading the crowd in the sinners' prayer Richard then gives them some basic instructions: start to pray to God every day in the name of Jesus Christ, read the Gospel of John everyone has been given, and start to attend a Bible believing church. A large team of local counsellors come forward and record the contact details of everyone who has come forward, the cards will be given to local pastors who will follow up and invite people to church.

Once the counsellors have finished recording all the names Richard then prays one prayer of healing over the crowd. Details of the prayer and how to conduct this part of the meeting, which is vital, are at the back of this book. Many people come to the platform steps after the prayer and testify that Jesus Christ has healed them. The most dramatic cases are allowed onto the platform, after being checked by local pastors, and tell the crowd what Jesus has done for them.

**A counsellor records details of a man who
has responded to the Gospel.**

Standing by the Cross – sermon outline

Text: John 19 : 17 – 26

"And He, bearing His cross, went out to a place called the Place of a Skull, which is called in Hebrew, Golgotha,[8] where they crucified Him, and two others with Him, one on either side, and Jesus in the centre. Now Pilate wrote a title and put it on the cross. And the writing was: JESUS OF NAZARETH, THE KING OF THE JEWS. Then many of the Jews read this title, for the place where Jesus was crucified was near the city; and it was written in Hebrew, Greek, and Latin. Therefore the chief priests of the Jews said to Pilate, "Do not write, 'The King of the Jews,' but, He said, "I am the King of the Jews." Pilate answered, "What I have written, I have written." Then the soldiers, when they had crucified Jesus, took His garments and made four parts, to each soldier a part, and also the tunic. Now the tunic was without seam, woven from the top in one piece. They said therefore among themselves, "Let us not tear it, but cast lots for it, whose it shall be," that the Scripture might be fulfilled which says: "They divided My garments among them, and for My clothing they cast lots. "Therefore the soldiers did these things. Now there stood by the cross of Jesus His mother, and His mother's sister, Mary the wife of Clopas, and Mary Magdalene[6] When Jesus therefore saw His mother, and the disciple whom He loved standing by, He said to His mother, "Woman, behold your son!"[7] Then He said to the disciple, "Behold your mother!" And from that hour that disciple took her to his own home. After this, Jesus, knowing that all things were now accomplished, that the Scripture might be fulfilled, said, "I thirst!" Now a vessel full of sour wine was sitting there, and they filled a sponge with sour wine, put it on hyssop, and put it to his mouth. So when Jesus had received the sour wine, He said, "It is finished!" And bowing His head, He gave up His spirit."

Introduction:

- The most dramatic and important moment in history, the death of Jesus.
- Different groups of people were there, different attitudes.
- Those same attitudes are represented here tonight.

Pontius Pilate

- Roman governor who had power of life and death.
- Considers the accusations against Jesus.
- Three times he says, "I find no fault in this man."
- His wife warns him not to have anything to do with Jesus.
- Pilate offers them a choice – Barabbas or Jesus.
- Pilate chooses to follow the crowd and release Barabbas.
- Pilate was a "convinced coward."

The Religious People

- Very religious, followed all the rules and regulations.
- They hated Jesus because he said he was the Son of God.
- Religion cannot save us from our sins.
- They were very proud and self-righteous.
- They had seen the miracles Jesus did but refused to believe in Him.
- Don't trust in your religion because religion cannot save.

The Roman Soldiers

- Tough and brutal men, had executed many people, a normal day for them.

- They had no interest in Jesus on the cross.
- Only interested in the things that BELONGED to Jesus.
- Many people are like that today.
- People want blessings, healing, church weddings, Christian funeral.
- But not interested in Jesus and His death on the cross for our sins.
- Focus your attention on Jesus, not on the things that belong to Jesus.

The Passers By

- Example of two men passing by on their way home.
- They look up and see the crucifixion.
- They are sympathetic towards Jesus on the cross.
- But they do not come close to the cross, they hurry on home.
- Their interest in Jesus is only for a moment.
- They are more focused on other things, getting home for dinner.
- Many people are like that today, they never come to the cross.

The Women "Standing by the Cross"

- Finally the Bible tells us about people standing by the cross, where we all should be spiritually speaking.
- Mary the mother of Jesus was there. Represents the good people in this world.
- She was a good and holy person, chosen to give birth to Jesus Christ
- But she was also a sinner, as we all are. She needed to come to the cross.

- Good works cannot save you. Living a good life cannot bring forgiveness of sins. No matter how good you are, you need to come to the cross
- Mary Magdalene was also standing by the cross
- She had been deep in sin. Jesus cast seven demons out of her.
- She represents people who have fallen deep in sin.
- No matter how bad you are, no matter what you have done, there is forgiveness for you at the cross of Jesus Christ
- Jesus said: "I will never turn away anyone who comes to me."
- No matter what sins you have committed, you can come to the cross.

Conclusion

- Don't be a "convinced coward" like Pontius Pilate
- Don't be like the religious people, religion cannot save you.
- Don't be like the soldiers, only interested in the things that belong to Jesus.
- Don't be like the men passing by, sympathetic but never coming to the cross
- Be like Mary the mother of Jesus who represents good people.
- Be like Mary Magdalene, who represents those who have fallen deep in sin.
- Come by faith to the cross of Jesus Christ and receive forgiveness for all your sins.

Altar call and prayer

Chapter 4

"Sheep and Goats"

In a small town in central Pakistan a large crowd has gathered for a Christian "festival." Large carpets have been laid on the ground, and spotlights and a temporary platform erected. Local Christian singers and musicians have been leading a time of worship well over an hour. At around 8pm Evangelist Richard Gunning is invited to the platform, with his interpreter, a local schoolteacher, to share the good news of the Gospel of Jesus Christ.

Jesus goes back to Heaven

Tonight I want to share with you about the return of Jesus Christ to this earth. Listen carefully to what the Bible tells us in Acts Chapter 1 verses 8 – 11 (NKJV) Jesus gives the disciples His final words and is lifted up into heaven. As He is rising on the clouds two angels appear.

"But you shall receive power when the Holy Spirit has come upon you; and you shall be witnesses to Me in Jerusalem, and in all Judea, and Samaria, and to the ends of the earth." Now when he had spoken these things, while they watched, He was taken up, and a cloud received Him out of their sight. And while they looked steadfastly toward heaven as He went up, behold, two men stood by them in white apparel, who also said "men of Galilee, why do you stand gazing up into heaven? This same Jesus, who was taken up from you into heaven, will so come in like manner as you saw Him go into heaven."

These verses tell us about the day Jesus Christ left this earth and returned to Heaven. They also give us a clear message that Jesus will return again. As Jesus was lifted up into Heaven, two men suddenly appeared wearing white clothes. I believe that these two men were actually holy angels sent by God. The main job of angels in the Bible is usually to bring a message, and the angels had a message for the disciples, as they stood staring up into the sky as Jesus departed from them. Their message was simple and very clear: "Jesus Christ will return to earth, in the same way that you have just watched Him depart."

As we look around the world today, we can see that it is full of many problems: poverty, sickness, wars, pollution, hatred, fighting, and many other terrible things are happening every day. Every time we turn on our radios or televisions, every time we buy a newspaper, we read about something bad that has happened. We very rarely hear, or read, about good news. The world needs Jesus Christ to return and sort out the terrible mess men and women have made of this earth. When Jesus returns the Bible tells us that He will rule as King of Kings and Lord of Lords. He will sort out the terrible mess mankind has made of planet Earth. There will be no more sickness, no more fighting, no more wars, no more hunger, no more sorrow, and no more death.

Two Questions

Tonight I want to answer two very important questions about the return of Jesus Christ to the earth. The first question is this: What are the signs that tell us Jesus is coming soon? The second question is this: What will happen when Jesus Christ returns to earth? These are two questions which people often ask. Let's look at them in a bit more detail.

Question 1: What are the Signs?

What are the signs that Jesus said would indicate that He is coming soon? The disciples asked this very question Matthew Chapter 24 and verse 3 (MEV): *"Tell us, when will these things be, and what will be the sign of Your coming and of the end of the age?"* Jesus then started to answer their question in some detail and listed several things that we should be looking out for as a warning that His return was getting closer. Now let me make it very clear that nobody knows the day or the hour when Jesus will come back, but these signs certainly give us an indication. If you set out on a journey to another town, usually you will see road signs that tell you how far away it is. As long as you are heading in the right direction, the distance will gradually get smaller on each sign. These road signs send us a message, they tell us we are getting closer to the place we are going to. In the same way, the signs that Jesus spoke about also serve as a warning to us that He is coming soon.

False Prophets

Jesus told the disciples that false prophets would arise. They would deceive many people into following them and believing their message. Be careful of anyone who tells you that there is another way to God without Jesus Christ. Today you will hear many people telling you, "all religions lead to God." But this is not correct, all religions do not lead to God. There is only one way to God and that is through faith in Jesus Christ. Jesus Himself said: *"I am the way, the truth, and the life. No one comes to the Father except through Me."* (John 14 : 6 MEV)

But today there are many false teachings, many false prophets, many wrong ideas about the how to get right with God. We need to be careful. If anyone is teaching something different to what Jesus clearly tells us in the Bible, then that person is a false prophet, and Jesus warned us about them.

Wars and Rumours of Wars

Jesus also gave them another sign, He said that there would be "wars and rumours of wars." The experts tell us that the frequency of wars is rapidly increasing, especially over the last 150 years or so. Since 1914 we have seen two terrible world wars, millions of people were killed. Even over the last 50 years there have been many terrible wars. It almost seems that as soon as one conflict is resolved then another one breaks out. Television companies send their reporters from one war zone to the next one.

It is terrible to see these things happening and Christians should be people of peace, Jesus said "Blessed are the peacemakers." We are also told that we should be people who pray for everyone who is in authority over us. We should pray for kings and presidents, Prime Ministers, and governments. We should pray that God will give them wisdom to rule over us wisely and well. But the sad fact is that there are many wars and rumours of wars, and these things are a sign that the return of Jesus is getting closer.

Famines, Epidemics and Earthquakes

Jesus listed three more signs to the disciples: famines, epidemics, and earthquakes. You don't need me to tell you that we see these things happening in many places today. The population of the world is growing very quickly, there are now more than 8 billion people on the earth. This rapid rise in population is causing a lot of problems and one of them is famines. It is terrible to see little children starving and without food.

Recently the world was hit by the Covid 19 pandemic. Almost the whole world was affected by this terrible virus, countries had to largely shut down. But there have been other pandemics in the last hundred years, such as Spanish flu, Zika, and Ebola. Jesus clearly told the disciples these things would happen, and the Covid 19 pandemic is the most serious to hit the world so far. I believe that in the future we will see more viruses hitting the world like this.

Earthquakes were another sign that Jesus mentioned. The experts tell us that in recent years earthquakes have been increasing, in both their strength and their frequency. We should not be surprised by these things, because Jesus warned that they would happen before He returned to earth.

The Final Sign

In many churches you will hear preachers talk about the different signs I have just mentioned to you. However, there is one more sign that Jesus is waiting for, before He comes back. This sign is often overlooked, and sometimes not even mentioned when people talk about the signs of Jesus return. In

Matthew Chapter 24 and verse 14 (MEV) Jesus gives us the final sign before His return: *"And the gospel of the kingdom will be preached throughout the whole world as a testimony to all nations, and then the end will come."* Jesus makes it very clear that everyone must first have an opportunity to hear the gospel, at least once, before He can return. The gospel must be preached to all tribes and ethnic groups before Jesus will come back. That is why we are having this meeting tonight. That is why thousands of evangelists and missionaries all over the world are preaching the gospel every single day. We want to see this final sign fulfilled so that the heavens can open, and Jesus returns and sorts out all the problems on planet earth. As soon as everyone has heard the gospel, then Jesus will return. This is the final sign that Jesus gave the disciples. He told them that when this had been done, "then the end will come."

Question 2: What will happen when Jesus comes back?

The day is coming when Jesus Christ will return to earth, the Bible clearly tells us this. When Jesus came the first time He was born in a stable, not many people knew that the Saviour of the world, the Son of God had come to earth and been born in Bethlehem. But when Jesus returns, He will not come quietly. No! the Bible tells us: *"For as the lightning comes from the east and flashes to the west, so will be the coming of the Son of Man."* (Matthew 24 : 27 MEV) Jesus himself tells us *"they will see the Son of Man coming on the clouds of heaven with power and great glory."* (Matthew 24 : 30 MEV) When Jesus comes back it will be a great event which everyone will see.

Then what will happen? What will happen to you, and you, and you? What will happen to me and to all of us? Well the

Bible clearly tells us that when Jesus returns to earth He will sit on a great throne and all the nations of the earth will be brought before Him. We will all be there, we will all appear before Him. Then what will happen, to you and to me? What will happen to us? Are you ready for that day?

Two Groups

The Bible says that we all be divided into two groups, just as a farmer separates his sheep from his goats. Did you notice that He does not separate good sheep from bad sheep. No, he separates two different kinds of creatures. The sheep, in this illustration in the Bible, represent the people who believe in Jesus. The goats represent the people who did not believe in Jesus and who never asked Him to save them from their sins. When you ask Jesus to come into your life and save you from your sins He changes you, spiritually speaking, from a goat to a sheep. You become a new creature, you receive a new nature, you receive forgiveness of sins.

Jesus Himself clearly tells us that there are only two possibilities on that day. We will each be brought before Him and then we will hear His decision about where we will spend eternity. Firstly Jesus will turn to a large group of people who are standing on his right. They are the people who believed in Jesus in this life. They are the people who accepted Him as their Lord and Saviour. They are the people who made that decision in this life before Jesus comes back. Jesus will turn to those people, and He will say: *"Come you blessed of My father, inherit the kingdom prepared for you since the foundation of the world."* (Matthew 25 : 34 MEV) Then those people will all go to a wonderful eternal life in the Kingdom of God forever. What a wonderful day that will be for all those people who have believed in Jesus in this life.

Terrible Words

Then Jesus will turn to the people on his left, people who did not believe in Jesus in this life, who never asked Him to be their Saviour. They will hear some terrible words. Jesus will say to them: *"Depart from me you cursed, into the eternal fire, prepared for the devil and his angels!"* (Matthew 25 : 41 MEV) What a terrible day that will be for everyone who has never accepted Jesus as their Lord and Saviour. Then those people will be thrown into that terrible lake of fire, prepared for the devil and his angels. God does not want you to go there, that is not His will for your life. The Bible tells us *"God is not willing that any should perish, but that all should come to repentance."* (2 Peter 3 : 9 KJV) God does not want you to go to that terrible fire. God did not prepare that fire for men and women. The Bible says that it was prepared for the devil and his angels. But only Jesus can save you from that fire. You don't have to go there, if you will only believe in Jesus and accept Him as your Saviour now, before He returns.

Let me ask you a question here this evening. If the heavens above us should open right now, and Jesus Christ returned from Heaven, and He came and sat on a great throne here in this place. If the holy angels of God then began to separate us into two groups, which side would you be on? Would you be with the believers in Jesus, would you be with all the people who have accepted Him as their Lord and Saviour, or would you be on the other side, with the people who never believed, who never accepted Jesus as their Saviour? Which side would you be on, on that great and terrible day? Please ask yourself that question right now, in your own heart? There is no place in the middle, you will either be on one side or on the other side. The choice you make about Jesus Christ in this life will decide where you spend eternity.

The VIP

If you were told that a king, or a president, or some other very important person (VIP), was coming to your house, you would make things ready. You would clean your house. You would put on your best clothes. You would tidy up any rubbish outside your house. You would do all you could to be ready for the arrival of someone very important. You would not wait until that important person was at the door before you started to prepare, no – you would prepare well in advance.

Let me tell you, someone far more important than any earthly king or president is coming soon. Jesus Christ is the King of Kings and the Lord of Lords and He is coming soon, and you need to be ready! There is a day coming when every person will bow their knee to King Jesus. The Bible tells us that: *"at that the name of Jesus every knee should bow, of those in heaven and on earth and under the earth."* (Philippians 2 : 10 MEV) There is a day coming when every knee will bow to King Jesus. But only those who recognised Him as king and accepted Him as their saviour will be allowed into His kingdom. Everyone else will still bow their knee but will then be cast into the lake of eternal fire.

Are You Ready?

So what about you tonight? Are you ready to meet the King of Kings? Are you ready for the day of judgement? Are you ready to stand before His throne? I believe many of you have realised tonight that you need to prepare, you need to be ready for the return of Jesus. To be ready for the return of the King of Kings there are three simple things that you need to do.

Firstly, admit that you are a sinner, that you have sinned before God and done things that are displeasing to Him. We have all sinned, not just you! The Bible says, *"for all have sinned and fall short of the glory of God."* (Romans 3 : 23 NKJV) That simply means that nobody comes up to God's standard, nobody is good enough to enter Heaven in their own strength or power.

Secondly, believe in your heart that Jesus Christ is the Son of God who died for your sins and rose again. The Bible says: *"Believe on the Lord Jesus Christ and you will be saved."* (Acts 16 : 31 NKJV) Only Jesus can save you from your sins, only Jesus can give you eternal life, only Jesus can bring you to Heaven when you die. There is no other way to God. Jesus himself said *"I am the way, the truth, and the life. No one comes to the Father except through me."* (John 14 : 6 NKJV)

Thirdly, confess, or say out loud that Jesus Christ is now your Saviour and your Lord. You can do that here tonight, you can confess with your mouth that you now believe in Jesus Christ. The Bible says, *"If you confess with your mouth the Lord Jesus and believe in your heart that God has raised Him from the dead, you will be saved."* (Romans 10 : 9 NKJV) Those three simple steps will make you ready to meet Jesus when He returns to earth. It is a s simple as A, B, C – ADMIT, BELIEVE, CONFESS. (That phrase can only be used if you are preaching to an English-speaking audience.)

The Appeal

Tonight I have told you about the signs that tell us Jesus is coming soon: wars and rumours of wars, false prophets, earthquakes, famines, pandemics, and the worldwide preaching of this Gospel of Jesus Christ. Just as road signs warn us that we are getting closer to our destination, so these different signs warn us that the return of Jesus Christ is getting closer.

I have also told you what will happen when the heavens open, and the King of Kings returns to this earth. He will sit on a great throne and all the people of the world will be brought before Him. This time He will not come as the Saviour of the world, this time He will come as the righteous and holy judge of every single man and woman. We will be divided into two separate groups, only two, with no place in the middle. Those who have believed in Jesus in this life will go to a wonderful eternal life forever in Heaven. But the people on the other side, the ones who did not believe in Jesus will be cast into a terrible lake of fire, prepared for the devil and his demons.

Where will you spend eternity? Are you ready for the return of Jesus Christ? If the heavens should open right now, in this meeting, and Jesus came back and we were divided into two groups, which side would you be on? Ask yourself that question right now. Nobody knows exactly when Jesus will come back, the Bible says nobody knows the day or the hour. But all the signs tell us that He is coming soon. Are you ready? What about you, and you, and you?

Let us all stand to our feet, we are going to pray. This is the most important moment in the meeting tonight. For many of you this will be the most important moment in your life. You now have to make a decision. You now have an opportunity to prepare yourself for the return of Jesus Christ, the Son of God, to this earth. This is the time for you to choose which side you will be on, on that great and terrible day of judgement when Jesus sits on His throne with the angels all around Him. Whilst every head is bowed and every eye is closed, let me ask you this question right now: How many of you here tonight want to ask Jesus Christ to save you from your sins and make you ready for the day when He returns? How many of you want to believe in Jesus tonight, let me see your hand right now! Lift your hand and wave it at me, all of you who want to accept Jesus Christ this evening.

All around the ground hundreds of hands are raised and are waving in the air. Richard then asks everyone who has raised their hand to come to the area in front of the platform. A team of trained and uniformed counsellors are ready to assist them. People quickly start to walk to the front, some are running. Within a couple of minutes a large crowd of people are gathered in front of the platform. Richard then leads them in a simple prayer of salvation, which they repeat out loud after the local interpreter. This prayer is found on page 133 of this book. Richard then gives them three basic pieces of advice: begin to pray to God every day, start to read the Bible or the copy of John's Gospel everyone is given, and start to attend a Bible believing church to learn more about Jesus and the Christian life.

Once the counsellors have finished recording all the names Richard then prays one prayer of healing over the crowd. Details of the prayer and how to conduct this part of the meeting, which is vital, are at the back of this book. Many people come to the platform steps after the prayer and testify that Jesus Christ has healed them. The most dramatic cases are allowed onto the platform, after being checked by local pastors, and tell the crowd what Jesus has done for them.

A typical altar call in Asia

Sheep and Goats – sermon outline

Text: Acts 1 : 8 – 11

"But you shall receive power when the Holy Spirit has come upon you; and you shall be witnesses to Me in Jerusalem, and in all Judea, and Samaria, and to the ends of the earth." Now when he had spoken these things, while they watched, he was taken up, and a cloud received Him out of their sight. And while they looked steadfastly toward heaven as He went up, behold, two men stood by them in white apparel, who also said "men of Galilee, why do you stand gazing up into heaven? This same Jesus, who was taken up from you into heaven, will so come in like manner as you saw Him go into heaven."

Introduction:

- Verses tell us about the day Jesus went back up into Heaven.
- They also tell us He will return in the same way He departed.
- World has many terrible problems. Man cannot solve them.
- When Jesus returns, He will fix everything, and He will rule as King of Kings.
- Tonight we will answer two important questions about the return of Jesus.
- Question 1: What are the signs that tell us he is coming soon?
- Question 2: What will happen when Jesus comes back to earth?

Question 1
What are the signs that tell us Jesus is coming soon?

- Signs are like road signs – destination is getting closer.

1. **False prophets – tell you there is another way to God without Jesus Christ**

- Jesus said "I am the way, the truth, and the life. No one comes to the Father except through me." (John 14 : 6)

2. **Wars and Rumours of Wars – wars have been increasing rapidly, especially over the last 150 years, two terrible world wars.**

- Christians should be peacemakers. We should pray for all our leaders.

3. **Famines, Epidemics and Earthquakes**

- Experts tell us that famines are also increasing, partly due to global warming.
-
- Epidemics are also increasing – e.g. Covid 19 affected the whole world.
-
- Earthquakes are increasing in both frequency and intensity.

4. **World Evangelism – this is the final sign.**

- Jesus said that when everyone has had a chance to hear the Gospel "then the end will come" – then He will come back.

Question 2
What will happen when Jesus comes back to earth?

- When He returns, He will not come quietly or secretly.

- The Bible says it will be as "lightning flashes from east to west."
- It will be a great event which everyone will see, not in secret.
-
- **We will be divided into two groups – no middle ground.**
- Separated like sheep and goats.
- Sheep are the believers – goats are the unbelievers.
- Believers will be welcomed into a wonderful eternal life forever.
- Unbelievers will be cast into an eternal fire, prepared for the devil and his demons.
- Which side will you be on, on that great day?
- If a VIP was coming to your house, you would prepare.
- At the name of Jesus "every knee will bow."

Summary

- Signs tell us Jesus is coming soon.
- Signs are like a warning – we should notice them.
- When Jesus returns, we will be divided into groups.
- Which side will you be on?
- Are you ready if Jesus should come right now, tonight?
- Get ready by doing these three simple things:
- ADMIT – that you are a sinner and cannot save yourself from your sins.
- BELIEVE – that Jesus died for your sins on the cross and that He rose again.
- CONFESS – say out loud, tell someone, that Jesus is your Saviour and Lord
- Get ready to meet the king of Kings when he returns!

Altar call and prayer

Chapter 5

Barabbas –
the one who got away!

In a church in Belfast, Northern Ireland a special evangelistic service is being held. The guest preacher is Evangelist Richard Gunning, the founder of "Reach the Unreached Ministries." After a time of praise and worship the senior pastor makes a short introduction and invites Richard to the platform to share the word of God.

Introduction

It's a great joy to be with you here today. I have preached the Gospel of Jesus Christ for over thirty years in many different countries, especially in Africa and Asia. It is amazing to see what God is doing around the world and how there is great revival in many places. I believe that the same revival will also come to the UK and to us in Northern Ireland. The Bible tells us that, *"there is no partiality with God"* (Romans 2 : 11 NKJV) that simply means that God has no favourites. What He does in one country He certainly wants to do in other countries, because He has no favourites.

Tonight I want to preach to you a message which I have entitled "Barabbas – the one who got away!" Let me read what the Bible says about this man Barabbas and the day he met Jesus Christ. If you have a Bible with you, please turn to Matthew Chapter 27 verses 15 – 26 (NKJV).

"Now at the feast the governor was accustomed to releasing to the multitude one prisoner whom they wished. And at that time they had a notorious prisoner called Barabbas. Therefore, when they had gathered together, Pilate said to them, "Whom do you want me to release to you? Barabbas, or Jesus who is called Christ?" For he knew that they had handed Him over because of envy.

While he was sitting on the judgment seat, his wife sent to him, saying, "Have nothing to do with that just Man, for I have suffered many things today in a dream because of Him." But the chief priests and elders persuaded the multitudes that they should ask for Barabbas and destroy Jesus. The governor answered and said to them, "Which of the two do you want me to release to you?" They said, "Barabbas!"

Pilate said to them, "What then shall I do with Jesus who is called Christ? "They all said to him, "Let Him be crucified!" Then the governor said, "Why, what evil has He done?"

But they cried out all the more, saying, "Let Him be crucified!" When Pilate saw that he could not prevail at all, but rather that a tumult was rising, he took water and washed his hands before the multitude, saying, "I am innocent of the blood of this just Person. You see to it." And all the people answered and said, "His blood be on us and on our children." Then he released Barabbas to them; and when he had scourged Jesus, he delivered Him to be crucified."

Two Little Boys

I want you to use your imagination for a few moments tonight. Imagine two boys who were born over 2,000 years ago. The first one was called Jesus, a name given to Him on the command of God His Father. In the book of Matthew the Bible tells us, *"You shall call His name Jesus for He will save His people from their sins."* (Matthew 1 : 21 NKJV) The other little boy was given the name Barabbas which literally means "son of the father."

As the boys got a little bit older their young lives started to go in different directions. The Bible tells us that Jesus was a good boy growing up who respected and honoured His parents. Luke Chapter 2 verse 51 (NKJV) tells us: *"He was subject to them... and increased in wisdom and stature and in favour with God and men."*

The Bible does not tell us anything about the childhood of Barabbas, the other boy we are looking at this evening. But it is very clear, from his later life, that he made some bad decisions.

Jesus continued from his early childhood to walk with God – that was a good decision. But Barabbas made some very bad decisions. He started to hate the Romans who had occupied his country. He became a rebel and a terrorist in his day, he allowed hatred and bitterness to fill his heart and his mind. He hated the Romans and thought that violence was the answer. He made a bad decision. Hebrews Chapter 12 verse 15 (NKJV) says: *"Looking carefully, lest anyone fall short of the grace of God, lest any root of bitterness springing up cause trouble and by this many become defiled."*

Life is all about decisions. Decisions have consequences, and decisions we make when we are young often have a powerful influence in shaping our lives and our futures. Young people here this evening, be careful what decisions you make in life because they will certainly impact your future. Choose carefully who your friends are, choose carefully who you decide to marry. Choose carefully what career or job you will do. Every day we are faced with decisions, some are big, and some are small.

Jesus, a man of action!

When Jesus was about 30 years old, He started His public ministry. Jesus was a man of action, always on the go, moving from place to place. He preached to large crowds, He healed the sick, He cast out demons. Jesus did many amazing miracles and taught many wonderful things. He preached love and peace, as well as repentance and faith in God.

Barabbas, the terrorist leader!

The life of Barabbas as a young man went in a very different direction. In one way he was like Jesus, in that he was clearly a man of action. Unlike Jesus, his heart was filled with hatred and bitterness. Unlike Jesus, Barabbas was not a man of peace. He wanted to drive the hated Romans out of his country, and he joined together with other men who wanted to fight the Romans. The Bible tells us that Barabbas had committed murder. Perhaps one night a couple of Roman soldiers were on patrol in Jerusalem and Barabbas and some of his men had ambushed them and killed them. Maybe Barabbas felt he was doing a good thing, fighting for freedom from the hated occupiers of his country.

However Barabbas has not gone unnoticed by the Romans, they know who he is and what he has done. They know he is a terrorist leader who has killed some of their men and they are out to get him. One night, as Barabbas lies asleep in his bed, the front door is broken down and Roman soldiers rush in.

"Barabbas!" they shout, "You are under arrest for the murder of Roman soldiers!" Barabbas is taken away to the Roman headquarters in Jerusalem and thrown into a prison cell. Two other men are also in that dark prison cell, two thieves who have been arrested earlier in the day.

The sentence is death!

The next day Barabbas and the two thieves are brought before Pontius Pilate, the Roman governor who will decide their fate. All of them know that they can expect no mercy from Pilate, a hard and brutal man who was there to enforce Roman rule and Roman law. Pilate listens to the charges against all three men, the trial is a quick one and Pilate then pronounces the sentence upon them: "All three of you will be crucified in a few days' time!" Terrified, all three men are roughly led back to that dark prison cell, deep in the basement of Pilate's headquarters.

The next day a crowd arrive at the gates of Pilate's headquarters in Jerusalem. They have a prisoner with them who has already been badly treated. The crowd are led by their religious leaders who are demanding that the prisoner, Jesus Christ from Nazareth, be sentenced to death. Pilate listens carefully to their accusations, then he stands up and says: *"I have found no fault in this man concerning those things of which you accuse Him…nothing deserving of death has been done by Him."* (Luke 23 : 14 – 15 NKJV) But the crowd are not satisfied and continue to demand that Jesus should be crucified. Then Pilate has an idea which he hopes will solve this problem. At that particular time of year there was a custom that one man condemned to death should be set free. Pilate decides to offer the crowd a choice, Jesus Christ or that terrible terrorist leader Barabbas. Surely, they will want Jesus to be freed, how could they possibly want Barabbas? But the crowd begin to shout loudly, "We want Barabbas!" Pilate is afraid of the reaction of the crowd, so he tells his soldiers to release Barabbas and to crucify Jesus Christ.

"You are free!"

Down in that terrible, dark prison cell Barabbas sits with the two other prisoners, waiting for the soldiers to come and crucify all three of them. They hear the soldiers coming in the corridor outside the cell. The key turns and the door unlocks. The soldiers roughly grab the first prisoner and drag him outside and place a large wooden cross on his back, to carry to the place of execution. Then the soldiers grab the second prisoner and also place a large cross on his back. Barabbas knows that now they will come for him as well, but a Roman officer comes into the cell and shouts at Barabbas: "Get out of here Barabbas, you are a lucky man today!" Barabbas wonders what is happening, is this some kind of a trick or a joke? Are they really going to let him just go free? "What has happened?" Barabbas asks the officer. "Are you really letting me go free?" The officer turns to him and says words that Barabbas will never forget: "Oh yes, you are free, Jesus Christ, the miracle worker from Galilee, is taking your place today. Pilate says we are to set you free." Two soldiers roughly grab Barabbas and march him to a side gate that leads out onto the street. They open the door and push Barabbas out. "Get out of here Barabbas, don't let us catch you again or you will end up nailed to a cross!"

Barabbas is the only person that Jesus, physically speaking, took the place of. He literally took the place of Barabbas, the murderer and terrorist leader. That third wooden cross had been made for Barabbas, but at the last minute Jesus took his place and Barabbas was free to go. But spiritually speaking, on the cross 2,000 years ago, Jesus took the place of everyone in the whole world. Jesus died for you, and you, and you. He died for me and everyone who has ever lived if we will only believe it and receive His forgiveness.

On the street

We don't know exactly what happened to Barabbas after he was set free, but I can just imagine that Barabbas starts to walk up the street and turns a corner. Suddenly he sees crowds are lining either side of the main street. A large number of Roman soldiers are pushing back the crowds. Three men are stumbling slowly up the street, each man is carrying a heavy wooden cross on his back. Roman soldiers are shouting and swearing at them, urging them to hurry up. The procession is heading towards Golgotha, the place of the skull, where the crucifixions are carried out. Barabbas pushes through the crowd, people make way for him, he is a well-known and much feared man in Jerusalem.

The three condemned men are passing by. Barabbas stares at the first man and immediately recognises him as Jesus Christ, the preacher from Nazareth. Barabbas has heard Him preach, but he didn't like His words about repentance and forgiving your enemies. No, that did not appeal to a fighter and rebel like Barabbas. Barabbas looks at Jesus and suddenly their eyes meet. Jesus looks at Barabbas with love in His heart. Suddenly Barabbas realises, "He is dying for me! He is dying in my place! That cross was meant for me, but He took my place!" Suddenly the hard heart of Barabbas starts to melt when he understands that Jesus is taking his place.

On the hill

In my imagination, Barabbas follows the crowd up the hill to Golgotha. There the soldiers drive nails into the hands and feet of the three prisoners and raise the crosses up high. Blood is flowing from their wounds. Many in the crowd are mocking Jesus and shouting: "If you are the Son of God, save yourself. Come down from that cross and we will believe in you!" But Barabbas knows in his heart that Jesus is dying in his place. He is also dying in your place, in my place, He is dying for the sins of the world. Think about that for a moment, Jesus is dying for you, and you, and you!

We don't know what happened to Barabbas, the Bible doesn't tell us. Did he repent of all his sins and understand what Jesus was doing on the cross? Did his life turn around, or did he go back to his old ways of hatred and violence? But, one day he will have to give an account. One day we will all have to give an account. The Bible tells us: *"At the name of Jesus every knee should bow… and that every tongue should confess that Jesus Christ is Lord, to the glory of God the Father."* (Philippians 2 : 10 – 11 NKJV)

Conclusion

When the door of that prison cell opened, and the Roman officer told him he was free to go, Barabbas gladly took the pardon that was being offered to him. He believed the words of that Roman officer and got out of there as fast as he could. He willingly believed the message the officer gave him, that someone else was going to take his punishment and die in his place. This was good news to Barabbas, he did not hesitate to receive the forgiveness he was now being offered.

But what about you tonight? You see I have told you tonight that Jesus Christ took your place. Tonight you can go free, tonight you can escape the punishment you rightly deserve for all your sins. Tonight you can have peace with God and know that your sins are forgiven. All you have to do is to believe it and to receive it. Forgiveness of sins cannot be earned by

Richard Gunning preaching recently in Northern Ireland

doing good deeds. Forgiveness of sins cannot be gained by following a religion and doing many religious things. No! You receive forgiveness of sins by believing that Jesus Christ died in your place on the cross, over 2,000 years ago.

These two young men, Jesus Christ and Barabbas, made different choices in life. One made good choices and the other made bad choices. But in many ways, we are all like Barabbas, we have all sinned. Maybe you are not as bad as Barabbas, but you have certainly sinned. The Bible tells us: *"All have sinned and fall short of the glory of God."* (Romans 3 : 23 NKJV) We have all sinned, in one way or another, we all deserve to be punished, and the Bible tells us: *"The wages of sin is death!"* (Romans 6 : 23 NKJV) Spiritually speaking, we all sit in that condemned cell, waiting to be punished for our sins. But the good news tonight is that Jesus Christ died for you, He took your place. Now you must believe it, now you must receive it and say: "Thank you Jesus for dying for me, thank you for taking my place. I believe in you Jesus, I believe you are the Son of God and the Saviour of the world." There is a way of escape tonight, there is a way to be forgiven, there is a way back to God, and it is by faith in Jesus Christ tonight.

The Appeal

Right now I ask you to stand to your feet. Let us all be quiet for a few moments in the presence of Almighty God. Tonight you have heard the Gospel of Jesus Christ. Deep in your heart you know that you are a sinner. Deep in your heart you know that you are guilty. Deep in your heart you want to find forgiveness and peace with God. Tonight you must believe that Jesus took your place and took your punishment. Then you will be free, then there will be no more condemnation for you, and you will have "peace with God through our Lord Jesus Christ." So right now, whilst every head is bowed and every eye is closed, and you want to receive Jesus as your Saviour, please just raise your hand in the air, let me acknowledge it, then you may take it down again. Let me see your hand right now!

Slowly hands are raised in different parts of the building, not in huge numbers as in Africa or Asia. But people have been touched and people have responded to the Gospel message. Richard asks the whole congregation to repeat together after him the sinner's prayer, which you can find on page 133 of this book. Those who have raised a hand are encouraged to speak to the pastor before they leave the building. Each one is given a booklet explaining the first steps of the Christian life and a New Testament.

Barabbas – the one who got away! – sermon outline

Text: Matthew Chapter 27: 15 - 26

"Now at the feast the governor was accustomed to releasing to the multitude one prisoner whom they wished. And at that time they had a notorious prisoner called Barabbas. Therefore, when they had gathered together, Pilate said to them, "Whom do you want me to release to you? Barabbas, or Jesus who is called Christ?" For he knew that they had handed Him over because of envy. While he was sitting on the judgment seat, his wife sent to him, saying, "Have nothing to do with that just Man, for I have suffered many things today in a dream because of Him." But the chief priests and elders persuaded the multitudes that they should ask for Barabbas and destroy Jesus. The governor answered and said to them, "Which of the two do you want me to release to you?" They said, "Barabbas!" Pilate said to them, "What then shall I do with Jesus who is called Christ? "They all said to him, "Let Him be crucified!" Then the governor said, "Why, what evil has He done?" But they cried out all the more, saying, "Let Him be crucified!" When Pilate saw that he could not prevail at all, but rather that a tumult was rising, he took water and washed his hands before the multitude, saying, "I am innocent of the blood of this just Person. You see to it." And all the people answered and said, "His blood be on us and on our children." Then he released Barabbas to them; and when he had [scourged Jesus, he delivered Him to be crucified."

Introduction:

- Two boys were born over 2,000 years ago.
- Jesus "He will save His people from their sins." Matthew 1 : 21

- Barabbas – means "son of the father".

Growing up:

- Jesus was a good and obedient son to Mary and Joseph.
- Barabbas – later life reveals he made some bad decisions.
- Barabbas started to hate the Romans, hatred and bitterness filled his heart, Hebrews 12 : 15.

Young men:

- Jesus was preaching, healing, casting out demons, raising the dead.
- Acts 10 : 38 "he went about doing good and healing all who were oppressed by the devil for God was with Him."
- Barabbas became a rebel leader, a man of violence, commits murder, arrested.
- Sentenced to death and thrown into the condemned cell.

The trial:

- Jesus is arrested and brought before Pontius Pilate
- Pilate says: "I have found no fault in this man." Luke 23 : 14 – 15
- Crowd asks for Barabbas, not Jesus, to be released.
- Barabbas hears the cell door open.
- Two thieves are brought out and given crosses to carry.
- But the centurion tells Barabbas: "You are free!"
- Jesus physically took the place of Barabbas.
- But spiritually speaking He took the place of everyone.

The Crucifixion:

- Romans take Barabbas to the gate and kick him out.
- Barabbas turns a corner and sees a crowd, three men are carrying crosses.
- Jesus looks at Barabbas, he realises "He is dying in my place!"
- Barabbas follows the crowd to Golgotha.
- Jesus is nailed to the cross as Barabbas watches. "He is dying in my place!"

Summary:

- Two young men
- Took different directions in life.
- We are all like Barabbas, "all have sinned."
- Spiritually speaking we are in the condemned cell unless we accept Jesus.
- We can be forgiven and go free spiritually if we believe in Jesus.

Altar call and prayer

Richard Gunning preaching in Sweden, with an interpreter.

Chapter 6

"The verse that says it all!"

In a church in Northern Ireland on a Sunday evening, Richard Gunning is the guest preacher at an evangelistic outreach meeting. After a time of praise and worship, announcements etc. the time has come for the preaching of the word of God. Richard is introduced by the pastor and comes to the platform.

It's a great privilege to be here with you this evening and to be asked to preach the Word of God. I love the Bible, I believe that it is different from any other book. One Christmas a few years ago, I was given a book about the famous Manchester United football manager, Sir Alex Ferguson, it was his autobiography. I like football, like many people here this evening, so I was very interested to read this book. It was a good book and I enjoyed it. He shared some interesting principles about man management and many other things about famous players, matches, winning trophies etc. However, I have never read that book again. I read it once and then I was finished with it. But the Bible is very different. I have read the Bible many times, from cover to cover, but every time I open it, I find something new, something I had not seen or realised before. You see the Bible says of itself in Hebrews Chapter 4 verse 12 (NKJV): *"The word of God is living and powerful, and sharper than any two edged sword."* No other book is like the Bible, no other book is living and powerful and able to speak to us like the Bible does.

This evening I want to speak about one of the best-known verses in the whole Bible. You may well have seen it on the back of buses. Not far from where I live, a farmer has written this verse, in huge letters, on the side of his barn. His property is close to a busy main road, so many cars see this sign every day. The verse I want to speak to you about tonight is John Chapter 3 verse 16 (NKJV): *"For God so loved the world that He gave His only begotten Son, that whoever believes in Him should not perish but have everlasting life."* Sometimes on televised football matches you will see someone hold up a poster with "John 3 : 16" written on it. This one verse sums up the main message of the whole Bible. If we were only allowed one verse to sum up the message of the Bible, this is the one most Christians and preachers would immediately think of. This evening I want to look at this verse in more detail, to break it up and try to explain clearly what God wants to say to us through this amazing verse.

For God…

The verse starts with God. Everything starts with God. The Bible begins in Genesis Chapter 1 verse 1 (NKJV) with these words: *"In the beginning God created the heavens and the earth."* God has always existed and God's plan to save men and women begins with God Himself. Many times men and women want to make up their own plan to somehow find their way to God, or to get right with God. I sometimes hear people say: "It doesn't matter what you believe as long as you are sincere." But when you think about it for a moment, that is absolute nonsense. Just because you sincerely believe something that does not make it true. For example, if someone sincerely believes that cows have ten legs and can fly, that does not make it true, no matter how sincerely they may believe it.

Sincerity of belief does not make something true, no matter how sincere the person may be.

The plan of salvation, getting our relationship with God sorted out and our sins forgiven, begins with God and not men and women. For centuries men and women have been trying to create their own plans of salvation, through different religious ideas and beliefs. There are many religions in the world today, and some of them teach some good things. But religion cannot save us and make us right with God. You see religion is the hand of man reaching up to God, trying to make contact with God, but it never works. The Gospel of Jesus Christ, which I am preaching to you tonight, is the hand of God reaching down to men and women to save us from our sin and the consequences of sin. Religion is something man does to try and reach out to God, but God has His own plan of salvation where He reaches down to us and saves us, if we will simply believe Him and trust Him.

The Bible is God's instruction book. It covers every area of life, both good and bad. It tells us about the very beginning of creation, how man got separated from God, how we can come back to God, and how Jesus Christ will return to earth at the end of the age. The plan of salvation for you and for me starts with God Himself.

So loved...

The verse continues and tells us that God, **"so loved"** the world. It doesn't just tell us that God loved the world but that He "so loved" the world, or that He so greatly loved the world. The Bible even tells us that not only does God loves us, but that He is love. 1st John Chapter 4 verse 8 (NKJV) says:

"God is love." When Jesus came to earth, He came to show us what God is like. Jesus said of Himself: *"He who has seen Me has seen the Father."* (John 14 : 9 NKJV) What kind of a God does Jesus reveal to us? Many people have the idea that God is some kind of angry old man up in the sky, and if you step out of line, He will hit you with a big stick. But Jesus reveals a very different kind of God to us. Jesus went about forgiving people whenever they came to Him in simple faith. When sick people came to Him, He stretched out His hand and healed them. When people who were possessed by evil spirits came to Him, He cast out the evil spirits and set those people free. When crowds of people came to hear Him preach and had nothing to eat, He took a little boy's loaves and fishes and fed the whole crowd of more than 5,000 people. Jesus revealed a God of love to us, a God who forgives, who heals, who sets free, and who meets physical and material needs as well.

That is good news for all of us. But the even better news is that the Bible clearly tells us: *"Jesus Christ is the same yesterday, today, and forever."* (Hebrews 13 : 8 NKJV) God loves you and He wants you to spend eternity with Him in Heaven forever. It doesn't matter how good you are, or how bad you may think you are, there is a place for you in Heaven. The Bible tells us that God *"is not willing that any should perish, but that all should come to repentance."* (2nd Peter 3 : 9 NKJV) Repentance is a word we don't hear very often these days, but it simply means to turn around. If you are driving somewhere in a car and you suddenly realise that you are heading in the wrong direction, you stop the car and you turn around, that is what repentance means. God simply wants us to recognise that we are headed in the wrong spiritual direction, to pause for a moment, and then to ask Him to save us, to turn our lives around and put us on the right road, the one that ultimately leads us to eternal life.

That He gave His only begotten Son…

The Bible tells us that God loved us so much **"that He gave His only begotten Son."** A sign of loving someone is to give something to them. We demonstrate our love for our husbands or wives, or our children, by giving them things. Things we give are a token of our love for the other person. The verse tells us that God gave His only Son. God sent Jesus to the world as a precious gift, to take the punishment for our sins so that we could go free and escape the punishment we fully deserved. You see you have sinned, and I have sinned. We have all done things that are wrong in the eyes of Almighty God, and a holy God must punish sin. But God loved us so much that He sent Jesus Christ to take the punishment we all deserve, so that we could go free.

Imagine you committed a terrible crime, and a judge sentenced you to death. You are taken to a prison and placed in the condemned cell to await the day and the hour when you will be put to death. That day soon arrives, and you hear the door to your cell being unlocked, your heart is beating, and a terrible fear grips your soul. But when the door opens the prison governor tells you that you are free to go, you will not be executed as planned! "How can this be?" you ask. But the governor tells you that someone came to the prison earlier in the day and offered to die in your place, so you are free to go. The price for your crime has been paid, the law is satisfied, and you can go free! Imagine how thankful you would be, that someone loved you enough to die in your place. But over 2,000 years ago that is exactly what happened! God sent His only Son to die in your place, in my place, in the place of everyone who will simply believe it and receive it with a thankful heart. The price has been paid, Jesus took your place, you can go free!

That whosoever...

The verse continues and tells us that this wonderful forgiveness, that Jesus paid for with His life, is for "whosoever." That means you and me. That means good people and bad people. That means people who are religious and people who are not religious. You see some people think that God is only interested in people who are very good, very holy, and very religious. But that is a very wrong idea. The Gospel is for everyone, the Gospel is for "whoever." The word Gospel literally means "Good News." It is good news for the person who has fallen deep in sin, it is also good news for the person who is religious and tries to live a good life. We all need to accept Jesus as our Saviour and receive forgiveness for our sins.

People put their faith in all kinds of things to try and get right with God. Some people trust in their religion, but religion cannot save us. When God wanted to save the world from sin, He did not send a religion, He sent His only Son! Good works cannot save us, living a moral life cannot save us, going through religious ceremonies cannot save us, that is why God sent Jesus. But Jesus came for everyone, Jesus came for "whoever!"

"Believes in Him..."

Jesus paid the price that was necessary to bring forgiveness of sins for everyone. But to receive this amazing and free forgiveness God asks us to do something, He asks us to believe. What are we to believe? We are asked to believe that Jesus Christ is indeed the Son of God, who came to earth and died for our sins, and who rose again from the dead. The Bible says: *"If you confess with your mouth the Lord Jesus and believe in your heart that God has raised Him from the dead, you will be saved."* (Romans 10 : 9 NKJV) We are asked to confess, or simply to say out loud, that Jesus is Lord, and to believe in our hearts that God has raised Him from the dead. The Bible tells us that if we do that, no matter who we are, then we will be saved. Saved from our sins and the punishment we deserve for our sins. This is something we all need, something we must all receive because we have all sinned and fallen short of God's standard. None of us can save ourselves, we all need a Saviour.

"Should not perish but have everlasting life."

The Bible makes it very clear that after we die there are only two possibilities. Either we will go to Heaven and spend eternity in the presence of Almighty God - Father, Son, and Holy Spirit, together with multitudes of angels and every person who has accepted Jesus as Lord and Saviour. Or, as Jesus Himself tells us, we will perish, we will go to a lost eternity and be cast into the everlasting fire prepared for the devil and his angels. (Matthew 25 : 41). There are only two possibilities, there is no middle ground, no third possibility somewhere in the middle, as many people seem to think. Your eternal destiny depends on your response to the death of Jesus Christ on a cross over 2,000 years ago. Jesus makes it very clear, either we will go to eternal life, or we will perish in that terrible fire which was prepared for the devil and his angels – not for men and women.

When I was a young man, I grew up in a Christian home. My parents were Christians, and I was taken to church every Sunday. But I was not right with God. I had never accepted Jesus as my Saviour. As I got older, I was very rebellious and started to live a sinful life, I was far away from God. If I had died as a young man, I would not have gone to everlasting life, I would have ended up in that terrible fire which Jesus warned us about. Then one night I read a book about this message which I have been telling you this evening. That only Jesus Christ can save us from our sins, and that we must personally ask Him to come into our hearts, to forgive us our sins, and to give us everlasting life. I prayed a simple prayer and asked Jesus to come into my heart and to save me from my sins. He answered my simple prayer, and my life began to change, day by day and year by year. For over 30 years now I have been travelling to many countries of the world, preaching this message, and many thousands have opened their hearts for Jesus and accepted Him as their Saviour.

The Appeal

So what about you tonight? You have heard the Gospel, so you have no excuses. You cannot say: "Nobody told me I needed to accept Jesus as my Saviour." This verse which we looked at this evening sums up the message of the Bible in just a few words. God loves you and He wants you to spend eternity with Him, He does not want you to perish, but to have everlasting life. But now you need to make a decision, now you need to make a choice. I ask everyone to bow their heads and to close their eyes just for a few moments. I will not embarrass you, I will not point you out, I will not drag you to the front. But I want you to do something very simple. I will count to three and when I say "three" I want all of you who want to accept Jesus as your Saviour, for the first time, to raise your hand. Let me acknowledge it, then you may take it down again, that is all we are going to do. Are you ready? One, two, three – let me see your hand right now!

Slowly, in different parts of the congregation, hands are raised, not in big numbers as in Africa or Asia. But people have been challenged and some have chosen to give their lives to Jesus Christ and to receive everlasting life. Richard asks the whole congregation to repeat together after him the sinner's prayer, which you can find on page 133 of this book. Those who have raised a hand are encouraged to speak to the pastor before they leave the building. Each one is given a booklet explaining the first steps of the Christian life and a New Testament. Richard then prays for the sick people.

"The Verse that says it all!" – sermon outline

Introduction
- Probably the best known verse in the Bible.
- Seen on the back of buses, on barns, on TV etc.
- This verse that sums up the message of the Bible.
- Let's break it down, line by line.

"For God…"
- Verse starts with God.
- Bible starts with God in Genesis 1 : 1.
- God's plan of salvation starts with God, not men and women.
- Sincerity of belief does not make something true, e.g. cows with ten legs!
- Religion cannot save us, hand of man reaching up to God.
- Salvation is the hand of God reaching down to us in the person of Jesus!
- Bible is God's instruction book. Reveals His salvation plan, starts with God.

"So loved the world…"
- Not just loved…but SO loved.
- 1 John 4 : 8 says *"God is love."*
- Jesus reveals God to us.
- Not a grumpy old man, but a forgiving, healing, saving God, meeting needs.
- Good news is that He is the same today – Hebrews 13 : 8.
- God wants us all to repent and to be saved – 2 Peter 3 : 9.
- Repentance means to turn around, e.g. turning a car around.

"That He gave His only begotten Son..."
- We demonstrate love by giving something, to wife, children etc.
- God gave Jesus to take the punishment we deserve for our sins.
- Example of a man condemned to death in prison, suddenly set free.
- Jesus took the punishment, we need to believe it and to receive it.

"That whosoever..."
- It is for whosoever – good or bad, it doesn't matter.
- Gospel means "good news" – for the wicked sinner, also the religious people.
- Religion or good works cannot save us, Jesus came for "whosoever."

"Believes in Him..."
- We must respond and receive God's gift of His Son.
- We must believe that Jesus died for our sins and rose again.
- Romans 10 : 9 – *"If you confess with your mouth the Lord Jesus and believe in your heart that God raised Him from the dead, you will be saved."*
- Confess simply means to say out loud, and then to believe in your heart that God raised Him from the dead.
- If we do that, we will be saved from our sins and the punishment for our sins.
- We cannot save ourselves, we all need a Saviour.

"Should not perish but have everlasting life."
- Bibles says there are only two possibilities after death.
- Everlasting life with God, His angels and all the people who believed.
- Or, the everlasting fire, prepared for the devil and his angels.

- No middle ground, as many people think.
- My personal testimony: rebellious young man, given a book by Billy Graham which explained the Gospel. I prayed a simple prayer, and my life began to change. I have travelled to many nations preaching this message.

The Appeal and prayer for the sick

Chapter 7

How to prepare a sermon

Introduction

The Bible tells us in Romans Chapter 10 verse 17 (NKJV) that: *"So then faith comes by hearing and hearing by the Word of God."* If you want to be a preacher and see results for your efforts, you must preach the Word of God. Today there is an increasing tendency for preachers to talk more about what Professor X, or Doctor Y, or Reverend Z wrote in his latest book. It is good to read faith building books and to try to increase your knowledge and understanding, there is nothing wrong with that at all. But when you read other books make sure that they agree with the Bible and are not trying to water it down and weaken it.

The apostle Paul wrote to his young disciple Timothy in 2nd Timothy Chapter 4 verse 2 (NIV): *"Preach the Word, be prepared in season and out of season, correct, rebuke and encourage with great patience and careful instruction."* Paul encouraged Timothy to "preach the Word!" Today there is a tendency to tell jokes and funny stories, quote different "experts" and water down the word of God. There is nothing wrong with telling a funny story at the at the start of your sermon, or in the middle of it, if it helps to illustrate a point, but your focus needs to be on the word of God.

The great American evangelist Billy Graham constantly quoted from the Bible in his evangelistic sermons. If you search the internet, you will find many of his sermons there. Billy

Graham regularly used the phrase "The Bible says..." His sermons regularly repeat that phrase, "The Bible says..." Billy Graham had huge success and hundreds of thousands came to the Lord in his great Gospel campaigns. His focus was always on the word of God, he preached the Bible and he preached and quoted often from the Bible in every sermon. Many thousands came to the Lord in his campaigns.

Feed on the Word

To be a preacher of the word of God you must feed upon the word of God. You must read your Bible diligently, from cover to cover. When you finish reading it, start again, read it over and over. I have read the Bible many times from cover to cover. I spend much more time reading the Bible than any other books. As I read the Bible my faith is built up and encouraged because "faith comes from the Word of God."

The Bible is unique amongst all books. It is the only one that has that unique ability within it to create faith in your heart. If you preach the Word of God, it will create faith in the hearts of those who hear you preach it. If you preach what the Bible says about salvation, then that will create faith in those who are listening to you to receive salvation. If you preach about divine healing and what the Bible says about it, then that will create faith in peoples' hearts to receive healing. If you preach about giving and tithing, that will also create faith in the hearts of people to give and to tithe and to trust the Lord to bless them in return, as He promises to do.

Get started again!

If you don't often read the Bible, let me give you some practical tips about how to get started again. In life people have good habits and they have bad habits. For example, smoking is a bad habit which can seriously damage your health. But because people have started smoking and continued with it, it has become a habit and they find it very difficult to stop. Brushing your teeth every day is a good habit, it helps to stop tooth decay. Most of us brush our teeth every day, it has become a habit. We try to teach our children good habits, because we know that if they get into the habit of doing a good thing then they will continue to do it, without our supervision. Bible reading is the same, if you discipline yourself at first, it will quickly become a habit and you won't need to push yourself to read it, it will become a good habit.

Bigger is better!

If you are not in the habit of reading your Bible, here are some things you can do to help you get started and develop a good habit. Firstly, buy a new Bible and make a fresh start. Buy one with big print that is easy to read. Many people have Bibles with very small print which is very off putting, before you even start. Just looking at many pages of tiny print that are hard to read will discourage you, before you even begin! Buy one with a large font size, at least 11-point size. The print you are reading right now on this page is 12-point print, hopefully you have found it easy to read! You can buy bigger than that if you wish.

Bibles are available up to 16 point which is pretty big but very easy to read, as you have just noticed! But 9 point is very small, like this, and many people are struggling to read Bibles with this size of print.

Try printing John Chapter 3 verse 16 several times on a piece of paper and increase the font size each time you type it, start with size 9 which is common in many smaller print Bibles. Then print it out and look at the different sizes of print and see which one works best for you and your eyesight. You really don't have to spend a lot of extra money to buy a bigger print Bible, unless you want a genuine leather cover or a study Bible.

Get started!

Now you need to get started and develop a Bible reading habit. Start in the New Testament. Have a pen, a ruler and a highlighter pen ready to use. Highlight with your highlighter pen anything that makes an impression upon you. Perhaps a promise, a command, a challenge. Write notes in the margin with a pen, underline with a ruler something that seems key to you. If a promise seems to jump out at you write the date beside it. Using a highlighter, a pen and a ruler will definitely help you to concentrate on what you are reading. Most Bibles have blank pages at the back and if there is something special that comes to you, write it down on those pages. As you read the Bible, it will slowly start to sink into your mind and into your heart, it will gradually build up your faith. When you start writing sermons you will find that verses you have read suddenly come to mind. Often when I am preaching, verses will just suddenly come to mind, verses I had not planned to use or written down in my notes. Those verses will not be in your mind and in your heart if you do not put them there by reading your Bible.

Set aside time!

Set aside regular time to read your Bible, the more you read it, the more you will want to read it. You will soon start to develop a Bible reading habit. Once you have finished the New Testament, start to read the Old Testament. Make notes, underline things, highlight things that strike you. Don't' worry too much about some of the difficult and heavy parts of the Old Testament, just read them any way and underline or highlight anything that seems important. Read it all, don't skip over any chapters or books, read your Bible from cover to cover.

When you have finished go and buy a new Bible and start again! I have done this many times. Sometimes I give the Bibles I have read away, to people in Africa when I go there to preach. Some people might think that is strange, especially as the Bibles are heavily marked and highlighted. But I would love to have a copy of a Bible used by a famous preacher and evangelist like Billy Graham. I would love to read his handwritten notes and insights! I am not comparing myself in any way to Billy Graham, I am just pointing out that some people like to get a Bible from a guest preacher.

Paul gave this instruction to his young disciple Timothy in 2nd Timothy Chapter 2 verse 15 (NKJV): *"Be diligent to present yourself approved to God, a worker who does not need to be ashamed, rightly dividing the word of truth."* Your foundation for writing sermons and being a preacher and an evangelist is to take good time to read the Word of God!

Pray and seek God!

If you want to be an effective preacher of the Gospel, you must be willing to pray much. In fact it is probably true to say that the more time you spend in prayer the more results you will see, and the more God will use you. John Wesley, the leader of the great Methodist revival in Britain in the 18th century, prayed for at least two hours every day, some accounts say four hours a day. He got up at 4am or 5am and spent hours in prayer. If you read about any preacher or evangelist who has seen great success you will find that spending time in prayer has been a key to their success.

The Bible says that the early disciples decided in Acts Chapter 6 verse 4 (NKJV): *"But we will give ourselves continually to prayer, and to the ministry of the word."* The Bible tells us that Jesus would on occasions pray all night. In the garden of Gethsemane, as He prayed before His arrest and subsequent crucifixion, He expressed His disappointment that the disciples could not stand with Him in prayer for one hour. Matthew Chapter 26 verse 40 (NKJV): *"Could you not watch with me one hour?"* I believe that an hour a day is the minimum we should be aiming for, especially if we are preachers of the Gospel. What price will you pay for success in ministry? If you are not prepared to spend much time reading your Bible and praying, maybe preaching is not for you?

"How can we pray for an hour or more?" many people will ask. Well, I can think of many things to pray about, here are just a few suggestions to help you get started.

- Thank the Lord for all His goodness and blessings to you and your family.
- Claim His protection over yourself, your family, your property, and your ministry.
- Pray for protection and blessing on all your co-workers.
- Pray for the people who pray for you and support you financially.
- Pray for unsaved family members, and people you know who need Jesus.
- Pray for your pastor and home church, for God to anoint and use them.
- Pray for your national and local political leaders.
- Pray for revival in your local area and nation.
- Pray for wisdom and guidance as you plan ahead.
- Pray and believe God for all the financial needs to be met in your life and ministry.
- Pray for any prayer requests that have been given to you.

Those are just a few things you can pray about every day. You will very quickly use up an hour and find that you need more time. You can also pray in the Spirit, in an unknown tongue or language. Ask the Lord to fill you with the Holy Spirit, if you have not yet been baptised in the Holy Spirit (Acts Chapter 2 verse 4). The more you pray the more you will want to pray, it will become a good habit, just like reading your Bible!

Understand the Difference between Preaching and Teaching!

If you study the ministry of Jesus, you will see two things: He was always PREACHING and TEACHING! I believe that these two things are the two "legs" God has given us to help the Gospel advance. Jesus used both of them consistently throughout His ministry, so did the disciples, just look at these verses, there are many more:

Matthew Chapter 11 verse 1 (NKJV): *"He departed from there to preach and to teach in their cities."*

Matthew Chapter 4 verse 23 (NKJV): *"He went about all Galilee, teaching in their synagogues and preaching the Gospel."*

Acts Chapter 28 verse 31 (NKJV): *"...preaching the kingdom of God and teaching the things which concern the Lord Jesus Christ..."*

Many people think that preaching and teaching are the same thing, but that is not correct, there is a big difference.

Preaching means to proclaim the Gospel to people who are unsaved and have not yet accepted Jesus as their Lord and Saviour. When we are preaching, we need to preach an evangelistic message, not a teaching message. I often hear ministers of the Gospel teach the church, then they add on an appeal for salvation at the end and wonder why there is rarely any response. To see people saved we need to preach, not teach, we need to preach an evangelistic message, focused on the unsaved people.

An evangelistic message needs to:

- **Let people see that they are lost in their sins and need to be saved.**
- **Explain clearly and simply how they can be saved.**
- **Tell them exactly what they need to do to be saved.**

If you are preaching, and people leave the meeting not having heard and understood these three things, then you have not been preaching, you have probably been teaching and you have failed to preach an evangelistic message.

Hundreds of pastors are inspired for evangelism in Kenya

Teaching means to train and instruct believers how to serve the Lord and how to spread the Gospel.
We need ministers who can teach the word of God, train believers how to live the Christian life, and teach them to spread the Gospel. The teaching ministry is absolutely vital, but we need both in the church today.

Some people are more naturally gifted and anointed as teachers, others as preachers and evangelists. Some people have a mixture of both in their ministry. I would say that my own ministry is probably 70% as a preacher/evangelist and 30% as a teacher. I know many ministers of the Gospel, some are 100% evangelists, some are 100% teachers, and many have a mixture of both, in varying degrees. I have seen other pastors who very rarely preach at all but who are wonderful pastors, anointed to care for people, visit and counsel them. The most important thing is to decide what God has called you to do and then stick firmly to that. If you are an evangelist, don't try to be a pastor. If you are called as a Bible teacher, don't try to be an evangelist. Don't step outside of your calling and try to be something God never called you to be.

We are all called to be "witnesses" and to share the Gospel when a suitable opportunity presents itself. But some people are certainly called to be evangelists, with a special ministry and anointing from God to effectively stand up and preach the gospel and see people respond and give their lives to Jesus Christ. Just as it says in Ephesians 4 : 11 (NKJV): *"And He Himself gave some to be apostles, some prophets, some evangelists, and some pastors and teachers."* I have heard people say, "we are all evangelists." We are certainly all called to be witnesses, but not everyone is called to be an evangelist, or a pastor, or a teacher, or a prophet, or an apostle.

PART 1 : PRACTICAL "DO'S AND DON'TS" IN PREPARING A SERMON

(1) Keep it logical!

You need to keep your sermon logical and easy to follow. I have heard it said that people think in straight lines. Don't jump around the Bible. Make sure the different verses you quote, and the various points you make, are all relevant to the topic and in a logical order. Don't go off on a tangent. I have heard many sermons where the preacher hopped about all over the place, making different random points, quoting different verses from different parts of the Bible, and not sticking to the subject or theme.

(2) Have Clear Points

Break your sermon down into clear points. If you read the sermons I have written earlier in this book, you will quickly see that I break them down into simple points. You will also see that I stick to the theme or subject and don't go off on a tangent, talking about something completely off the subject or irrelevant. For example, if you are going to preach about the second coming of Jesus, you could break it up by posing and answering three simple questions:

- Will Jesus come back to earth?
- What are the signs of His coming?
- What will happen when He returns?

It is a very good and simple system to have three or four questions, to pose them and then answer them. This will help you to keep on track and not go off on a tangent. It will make your sermon simple to follow and memorable to those who are listening to you. You can see how I have done this in my sermon in Chapter 4, "Sheep & Goats."

(3) It should be real to you

If you are going to preach about something, make sure that it is real to you. Quoting at length from a book, or a commentary someone else wrote, isn't real to you. Don't give them a lot of facts and figures that you read in a book or found on the internet. I heard someone some years ago say he was going to preach about the Bible. He then spent a lot of time giving a lot of facts and figures that anyone could have found in Wikipedia or on the internet.

Speak from the heart and with conviction, but it must always line up with the Bible. Giving your testimony is a good place to start but keep it logical and quote verses at regular intervals to back up what you are saying. For example, you could say: "When I accepted Jesus as my Saviour my life began to change." Follow that up by quoting, for example, 2nd Corinthians Chapter 5 verse 17 (NKJV): *"Therefore, if anyone is in Christ, he is a new creation, old things have passed away, behold all things have become new."* Then give a clear example of something in your life that changed when you accepted Jesus as your Saviour. Don't just tell people "Jesus can change your life!" That is absolutely true and that is fine, but why not tell them briefly how He changed YOUR life and base it on that verse? People are always curious about other peoples' lives, if you share something from your life it will make it much more real and memorable to people.

(4) Keep it practical

People like to hear something practical, something they can do as a direct result of listening to you speak. Be practical in what you say. I hope that in this book I am being very practical. It is of little value to tell people to "read the Bible." It will be of much more benefit if you tell them HOW to read the Bible and tell them how YOU read the Bible and what works for you.

Again you must base what you say on the Bible and quote relevant verses of Scripture, as I have explained above.

(5) Use examples and illustrations

When Jesus was preaching and teaching, He always used practical illustrations from everyday life. He constantly used parables to make His teaching real and understandable to people. Today many preachers fail to do that. Jesus used illustrations such as a farmer sowing seed, a landowner harvesting, a fisherman catching fish, light and darkness, and many more. He always illustrated what He was saying and teaching by using examples and illustrations from everyday life that people were familiar with and understood. In fact the Bible tells us in Mark Chapter 4 verse 34 (NKJV): *"He did not say anything to them without using a parable."* Always use illustrations from everyday life to illustrate your points, as far as it is possible.

(6) Lift up others!

Never use the platform to put other people down or make jokes about them or say something negative about them. Always lift people up, say something like: "Didn't the worship team do a great job today?" Even if you think someone in the congregation likes a joke and won't mind if you tell a story that makes them look silly or foolish, never try to put them down. I saw this quote on Facebook recently: "The only time you should look down on someone is when you are trying to lift them up!"

PART 2 : PRACTICAL PREPARATION

Pray and seek God!

When you start to prepare a sermon the first thing you need to do is to take good time to pray and ask God what He wants you to share. Seek to listen to the voice of the Holy Spirit speaking quietly to you. A passage or a subject may come to mind, that could well be what the Lord wants you to speak about. Learn to listen to the still, small voice of the Holy Spirit speaking to you.

Have a pen and paper handy and write down any thoughts, impressions, ideas, or verses that come to mind. If a particular topic or verse continues to come to your mind that is probably what you should speak about.

Preaching from a verse or passage of scripture

When I am preparing, I usually pick one of two types of sermons. The first one is often called "expository" preaching. This means taking a verse or a passage of scripture and explaining it or expounding it – opening it up and going into detail about the passage or verse. For example, I sometimes preach a sermon which is entirely based on John Chapter 3 verse 16 (NKJV): *"For God so loved he world that He gave His only begotten Son, that whoever believes in Him should not perish but have everlasting life."*

You have already read this sermon in Chapter 6 of this book, "The Verse that says it all!" I break the verse down into small sections and preach briefly on each part of the verse.

For God – I would speak about God as our creator and heavenly Father. How He created all things well in the beginning. His plan to save mankind from the consequences of sin.

So loved the world – I then speak about the love of God for every person. About how the Bible tells us that "God is love."

That He gave – A sign of love for others is to give. The Bible tells us that "God so loved the world that He gave…"

His only begotten Son – I talk about Jesus, the Son of God who died for us and rose again from the dead. I talk about how Jesus reveals God to us in the form of a man, His miracles, His healing power, His compassion.

That whoever – I then speak about salvation being available for everyone, no matter how bad they are, or what background they come from. Salvation and eternal life are for "whoever."

Believes in Him – I speak about the vital importance of believing, salvation is by faith, not by works, or good deeds, or following a religion.

Should not perish – I explain that only Jesus can save us from our sins and the consequences of sin, eternal separation from God in a place Jesus described as a lake of fire prepared for the devil and his angels.

But have everlasting life – I explain that the free gift of God is eternal life if we will believe in Jesus. I talk about how wonderful that eternal life will be and encourage people not to miss out on it.

I back up each section above with other verses that support what I am saying. I also share a little of my own salvation testimony, this makes it more personal and real to people.
Finally I challenge people to do exactly what the verse tells us to do – to believe in Jesus so that we shall not perish but have everlasting life.

This is just a very simple example of how you can take one evangelistic verse from the Bible and use it as a basis on which to preach your sermons. If you read the sermons I have given you earlier in the book, you will see that they are all based on one verse or a passage of scripture.

Preaching on a topic or a subject

If you decide to preach or teach on a subject, rather than a verse or short passage of scripture, that is absolutely fine too. Choose a subject you want to speak on and feel the Lord is putting on your heart. There are many subjects you can preach or teach on: faith, prayer, healing, the Holy Spirit, giving etc. etc. There are a huge variety of subjects you can choose from. But whatever subject you decide to preach or teach about, make sure that you stick to your subject, and make sure that every verse you quote relates to the subject you are talking about. If you think of a string of pearls on a necklace, the string is the theme of your message and the pearls are the different points, verses and illustrations you use, but they must all "hang" on the string, which is your theme or topic.

For example, if you are going to talk about faith then you can take examples and verses from many different places in the Bible.

- You could talk about Noah and how he acted in faith when God told him to build the ark.
- You could talk about Abraham believing God for a son, even though both he and his wife were very old.
- Then you can share a little bit about Joseph, and how he held on by faith to the vision God had given him, even though he ended up in a prison in Egypt.
- You can mention David and his faith when he went out to fight the giant Goliath, even though he was just a young shepherd boy.
- Then you can move into the New Testament, perhaps talk about Peter walking on the water in faith when Jesus told him to come to Him.
- Although you are taking different examples and verses from different parts of the Bible, they are all very relevant to your subject of faith. You can also give a couple of examples from your own life. Tell people about a time when you really had to trust God and you had to stand in faith. Tell them what happened and how God helped you or brought you through that situation. Always be honest when you share about something from your own life, never exaggerate or say something that is not accurate, in an attempt to make the story sound better or more exciting.

Start to assemble an order to your points.

Write down all the different thoughts, ideas, illustrations, and verses that come into your mind. Then start to assemble them into a logical order. It is a good system to break the different points up under the following subheadings:

Text: Read a passage of scripture or a key verse that you are going to talk about. If you are going to preach about a topic, rather than about a verse or passage, try to choose a verse which sums up what you want to say and use that as an opening text. I have used faith as an example of a topic you could speak about. If I was going to preach on the subject of faith I might use Hebrews Chapter 11 : 1 (NKJV) as my opening text: *"Now faith is the substance of things hoped for, the evidence of things not seen."*

Introduction: Tell people what you are going to talk about. For example in the sermon earlier in this book in Chapter 3 entitled "Standing by the Cross," I begin by telling people that we are going to look briefly at the different people who were standing around the cross of Jesus Christ, and their different attitudes to Jesus as He was hanging on the cross. So right at the beginning I have already given people a brief outline of what I am now going to speak about.

Main body: These are the main points which you wish to communicate with people. Make sure all your points, verses, and illustrations that you use are relevant to the subject.

Summary/Conclusion: Finally end your message with a brief summary of the main points you have just spoken about. This reminds people of all your main points and brings the message to a good conclusion.

If you watch any television news programme you will see that they always follow the same pattern. They start with the headlines, they tell you the main points that they are going to inform you about. Then they tell you each news story in much more detail. Finally they summarise what they have just told you, briefly repeating the main points. They have always used this format for as long as I can remember. Why? Because it is a proven and effective way of communicating with people. If there was a better way of doing it, then all the television companies around the world would be doing it!

Illustrate your points!

Always illustrate your points with simple illustrations. Jesus always used parables when He was speaking to crowds of people. He used illustrations from everyday life. He talked about farmers sowing seeds, about sheep and goats, about a lost sheep or pearl. He talked about light and darkness, wheat and tares (weeds), things ordinary people could understand and identify with. Matthew Chapter 13 verse 24 (NIV) says: *"Jesus spoke all these things to the crowd in parables, He did not say anything to them without using a parable."* If Jesus needed to use parables to help people understand what he was saying, then I guess we need to do the same?

Draft an outline

Start to write your outline for your sermon. You can write it by hand or use your tablet or laptop, it is up to you. I am a bit older than most of you reading this book, so I do mine by hand and use paper notes, which I attach inside my Bible with paper clips, but most younger people will probably use a tablet or laptop. Write your points out in bullet point style. Highlight key points in yellow, so that you don't miss them when you are preaching. If you are just starting out as a preacher, you might prefer to write the whole sermon out, word for word. That is fine, but as you gain experience try to move towards just using sermon outlines.

Richard's hand written notes inside his Bible, with a timer clock

NB: Always write out in full any verses you plan to quote. I have seen some inexperienced preachers make a terrible mess by trying to find different verses in their Bible and flicking through many pages in their Bibles whilst preaching. This will slow you down terribly and can even be embarrassing if you cannot quickly find the verse you are looking for.

You can use a laptop, tablet, or your smartphone if you prefer. If you are going to write your notes on paper then don't use loose sheets of paper for your notes, they can easily become mixed up. If you are preaching outside, they could even blow away! Instead use a wire bound A5 size notebook which you can buy very cheaply in any supermarket. A wire bound notebook will lie flat and you can easily turn the pages, in addition you will never need to worry about the batteries running out, or pages getting mixed up and falling on the ground!

Chapter 8

How to deliver a sermon

Key advance preparations

Once you have written your sermon and have prepared an outline, you are ready for the next step. There are some key preparations which you need to make in advance. Most of these things apply to preaching in both churches and open-air campaigns, but a few things are different, the key points now follow.

- Take time to preach the message to yourself in a private room. This is important, especially if you are not an experienced preacher. Preach your sermon out loud to yourself. I know a great young preacher in Northern Ireland who is drawing a fast-growing crowd to his church. He told me he sets aside every Friday to preach his sermon to himself - three times! This helps him to really get to know the message he is going to preach and to be very familiar with it.

- You should also time yourself to see how long it takes. Then you will know if you need to add more material, or to reduce it, if it is taking too long. As a rough guide, a sermon that is about 3,000 words long will take about 20 minutes or more to preach. Remember to allow some minutes for any opening remarks you may decide to make and also for the appeal at the end. This will bring you close to 30 minutes in total.

- Change anything that does not seem to work well.

Important tips for preaching in a church

- If you are going to speak in a church as a guest preacher, always check well in advance with the pastor how long you are allowed to speak for. If you are given a time limit, make sure you respect it.

- Check what the dress code is in that church and be sure to follow it. Make sure you know where the church is located, if you have not been there before. Check with the pastor what time he would like you to arrive at, ahead of the meeting.

- Check in advance with the pastor if you can use a PowerPoint to go along with your sermon. You can write out verses you will use on the slides or use pictures to illustrate your points. I usually write verses in a clear white font on a plain black background. Thousands of free to use images are available on the internet, just copy and paste them into your presentation. If you are not skilled at doing this, ask someone to show you how to do it.

- Make a printed copy of your outline and then write in red ink a slide number at the point in the sermon where each slide should be put up on the screen. I then give this copy of my outline to the sound person at the church and ask them to put up each slide at the relevant point in my sermon. I find this works very well for me and I then don't have to worry about the correct slide appearing at the right time or messing around with a "clicker" to bring the images up myself.

- Make sure you always save your PowerPoints, so you can use them again on a different occasion. Always keep your outlines in a file or on a memory stick.

Get up early!

- Get up early and take good time to pray before any meeting where you are the preacher. Pray in your own language and also in the Holy Spirit (tongues or your prayer language) which will build you up spiritually. Pray for God to move in the meeting, to save souls and heal sick people. Claim His protection over you, your family, and every aspect of the meeting.

- Make sure you have your Bible and your sermon notes or tablet etc. with you. You should also bring a bottle of water. You should also bring some method of timing how long you are speaking, perhaps on your phone, or buy a small timer which are easy to find online. Personally I use a small timer which I set on the lectern beside my Bible. I just press "start" as soon as I stand up to speak, this lets me know exactly how long I have been speaking for. It is much more convenient and easier than trying to look at my watch. If you rely on your watch, you may easily forget what time you started preaching at, therefore you will not know how long you have been preaching.

Be early at the church or venue!

- Always allow good time to get to the church or meeting venue, never be late or arrive at the last minute. Always arrive in good time for any meeting. If there is a prayer meeting before the service, make sure you attend it. Set a good example as a visiting preacher.

- If an offering is received during the service, make sure you contribute, again you will set a good example as a visiting speaker.

- Sit near the front, so that you are ready to get up when you are invited to come forward to preach. Remember any finishing time the pastor may have given you and make sure you stick to it. If you speak for a long time after the pastor had asked you to finish, then you are unlikely to be invited back again! You just showed the pastor that he cannot really trust you.

- During the time of praise and worship make sure that you join in. You should not be sitting with your eyes closed praying, or reading your notes, when the people are worshipping. That sets a bad example and suggests you think worship is not important. Join in enthusiastically and set a good example!

Before you get up to preach

- Clear your throat, if you feel you need to do so, or blow your nose. It is much better to do these things before you get up on the platform than to do them on the platform, just before you start to speak.

- Take a small drink of water before you are invited to the platform to preach. Have your notes etc. ready to go.

Richard preaching in a campaign in Africa

On the platform

- Take a moment to settle yourself, start your timer and place it where you can easily see it as you preach.

- Make sure the microphone you are using is switched on. If you have been asked to turn on a microphone yourself before speaking, wait for a second or two, so that you give the sound team a chance to turn up your volume at the sound desk.

Getting started

- Introduce yourself if nobody has introduced you. Say a few words about yourself and that you are happy to be here today.

- Make a positive remark about the church and thank them for inviting you to speak.

- Never put yourself down in any way or make a negative comment about yourself. You are there to preach the word of God. People will already have a measure of respect for you as a guest preacher, don't destroy that by making some sort of negative comment about yourself before you have even started to preach.

- Introduce your topic briefly, say something like: "Today I want to speak to you about the return of Jesus Christ to this earth. I want to answer three simple questions that many people have about this subject." Then read your Bible text and start to preach your main points.

Key points on your delivery

- Vary the speed and level of your voice. No matter how good your content is, people will get bored if you speak at the same level and speed and never vary it. I have heard some preachers who speak quite slowly and at the same speed for the whole sermon, that will be very boring for your listeners. I have heard preachers who also get up and talk very quickly and loudly for the whole sermon, that can also be boring because there is no variation.

- If you slow your voice speed down considerably at the end of some sentences it will help to grab peoples' attention. For example: "Some people try to tell us Jesus will never return. Have they got it right? I....DON'T....THINK....SO!"

- You can also help to keep peoples' attention by saying when you come to an important point: "This is a very important point, would you please lift your hand if you are listening!" Pause for a moment and give people an opportunity to raise a hand. Doing this will immediately refocus their attention if they have started to lose concentration.

- If you are confident, move around the platform, don't just stand behind the lectern the whole time. But if you are inexperienced and new to preaching, wait until you have a bit more confidence before you start to move around a bit on the platform.

- Discipline yourself to keep an eye on your notes, make sure you don't get side tracked.

- Keep an eye on your timer, so that you can shorten or lengthen your points, according to the time.

- Be careful to avoid annoying mannerisms or repetitive gestures. If the sermon has been recorded on video, be sure to watch it later. Carefully look at your speed and tone of voice, also look out for annoying or repetitive gestures and try to eliminate them next time you preach.

- As you become more confident as a preacher, try to move away from reading the sermon word for word, which is what most people do when they start as a preacher. Start using outline notes, you can find examples of my sermon outlines at the end of each of the sermons earlier in this book.

Closing

- Try to summarise briefly what you have said in the main body of your sermon. Remind people quickly of the most important points.

- Respect the time limit you have been given.

Preaching in an open-air campaign meeting

- If you are going to speak in an open-air campaign meeting, many of the things I have said above, about speaking in churches, also apply. However there are a number of differences which you need to be aware of.

- In most campaigns the open-air evangelistic meetings are usually in the evening, with daytime training seminars for pastors and local leaders usually held in the mornings. In the evening meetings the main focus is on preaching the Gospel to the many unsaved people who will be there. In the morning seminars the focus is on teaching and inspiring the pastors.

- In the evening meetings there will often be a long time of singing, praise and worship before the preaching. Try not to arrive too early at the meeting, so that you are not sitting around for a couple of hours waiting for the time to preach. Agree a time with the local organiser when he feels he needs you to be there and follow their advice.

- Make sure you bring a bottle of water with you, plus your notes and your Bible. I see some young preachers who have all their notes and a Bible on their phones, there is nothing wrong with that, but make sure your phone is fully charged.

- When you arrive at the campaign ground you will usually be shown to a seat beside the platform or on it. Be warm and friendly and shake hands with the various pastors and leaders who will be there.

- If possible, try to get a few minutes with your interpreter whilst you are waiting to preach. Tell them what you are going to speak about and tell them the main points. This will be a great help to them as they interpret.

- When you are invited to preach, go forward confidently, and take the microphone. Greet the crowd warmly and powerfully. Tell them what a joy it is to be with them and to share the good news of the Gospel with them. Then start to preach your sermon. I have given detailed advice about how to preach with an interpreter in the next chapter of this book.

- If you feel confident, move around the platform, and spend a few moments preaching to different areas of the crowd. But if you are new to preaching in campaigns it is fine to stay in one place, close to the lectern or table where you have your notes.

- If you are in a country where another religion is dominant, don't speak about that religion and definitely do not say anything negative or critical about it. You can easily create a lot of problems and stir up opposition. You can also create long term problems for the local pastors and leaders who live in the area after you have flown home. It is generally best to simply preach the Gospel and quote from the Bible. You should show respect for other people's religion and beliefs, even if you do not agree with them.

- In some countries there are "anti-conversion" laws, so do not use words like "convert" or "conversion." Just talk about "accepting Jesus as Saviour," or "asking Jesus into your heart." It is also fine to use words like "saved" and "born again." If you are not sure about these things check carefully with the local organiser, or an experienced evangelist if you are in a team.

- When you have finished your sermon, you need to make an altar call for salvation and then pray for healing for the sick people. Full details of how to do both these things are in Chapter 10 of this book.

Checklist for preaching in a church:

- Check the time allowed for preaching.
- Check the dress code and respect it.
- Check what time you should arrive at.
- Check if it is ok to make an appeal or pray for the sick.
- Get up early and pray.
- Bring a water bottle, Bible, notes, and a timer.
- Attend any pre-service prayer meeting.
- Give the sound person a copy of your outline, if using a PowerPoint.
- Give an offering if one is taken.
- Clear your throat and take a sip of water before getting up to speak.
- Thank the pastor for inviting you.

- Don't say anything negative about yourself or put yourself down.
- Vary your voice level and speed of speaking.
- Stick to the topic, keep an eye on your notes.
- Respect the time limit you have been given.
- Stay behind afterwards and be available to speak to people or pray for them.
- Keep a written record of every sermon you preach, where you preached it, and the date you preached it. This will stop you from using the same sermon if you return to a church or town some years later.

Check list for preaching in an open-air campaign meeting:

- Agree on an arrival time at the ground with the local organiser.
- Bring your notes, your Bible, and a bottle of water.
- Be friendly and polite on arrival, shake hands with local pastors and leaders.
- Try to share your outline with your interpreter whilst waiting to preach.
- Be confident right from the start.
- Follow the guidelines in the next chapter about preaching with an interpreter.
- Move around the platform, if you are confident doing that.
- Never criticise other religions or comment on their beliefs, just preach the Gospel.
- Be aware of local laws about "conversion."
- Make an altar call and pray for the sick, full details are in Chapter 10 of this book.

Chapter 9

Working with an Interpreter

If you are going to preach in other countries, you will often need to work with an interpreter in your meetings or campaigns. There are several important points I would now like to share with you which I believe will help you and any interpreter you work with.

- Try to meet with your interpreter before the meeting starts. Share your outline briefly with them and explain what your message is about. This will help them to understand the direction your sermon is headed and enable them to be more effective as they have a grasp of what you are trying to communicate to people.

- If you sense that the interpreter is inexperienced, do your best to reassure them. Tell them to just copy your tone of voice and hand gestures etc.

- Do not use English expressions which often do not easily translate into the language of your listeners. For example, I heard an American preacher in Norway a few years ago use the phrase "in the middle of nowhere." I have lived in Norway and have learnt the language, but that phrase did not translate easily into the Norwegian language. Please be careful with using fixed expressions when using an interpreter. You should also be careful with jokes and humour which can sometimes be difficult to interpret into another language.

- Don't speak a very long sentence at one time. For example, do not say, "It is wonderful to be here with you tonight. I come from Northern Ireland, which is very close to England, and I have travelled to many countries preaching the Gospel." It will be hard for any interpreter to remember all of that. Instead break it up into short sentences, with time for the interpreter to interpret each phrase, for example: "It is wonderful to be here with you tonight..........I come from Northern Ireland.........which is very close to England.......I have travelled to many countries preaching the Gospel."

- Try to make sure that each phrase or sentence is complete, don't leave the interpreter confused about what you are trying to say or what is coming next. Don't stop in the middle of a phrase or sentence, make sure it is complete, but without using long sentences.

- Tell your interpreter not to try and look up any verses you quote as you preach, but just to translate what you have just said. You will lose your flow if the interpreter starts trying to look up verses in his/her Bible.

- Always wait until the interpreter has finished speaking, before speaking your next line. I have seen preachers start to speak again before the interpreter has fully finished their sentence. Always wait for the interpreter to finish speaking. Something you say may take a little longer to say or explain in the local language. Remember in many more remote places the people do not understand English, so they are listening to the interpreter, not to you! It is really awful to see a preacher talking over the interpreter whilst they are still translating the previous sentence. It is not necessary to start speaking before the interpreter has finished speaking, and it can come across as rude and even arrogant to do so.

- Use short, simple phrases. Avoid difficult or rarely used English words. For example, don't say, "Joseph found himself in a terrible predicament." Just keep it simple and say, "Joseph found himself in a bad place."

Richard and his interpreter in Burkina Faso. Notice how the interpreter is copying Richard's gesture exactly.

- Never turn your back on the interpreter. I have noticed many times that if I turn my back on the interpreter it makes it much harder for them to hear what I am saying. Try to always stand sideways to your interpreter, or even to turn your head slightly towards them as you speak, so they can clearly hear what you are saying.

- If the interpreter does not understand something you say, repeat it using different words, do not just keep repeating the same words again and again. Clearly the interpreter has not understood a word you have used, you need to say it very quickly in a different way and using different, simple words.

- At the close of the meeting always make a point of thanking the interpreter and tell them they did a great job. It is good to encourage and uplift people.

Chapter 10

Altar Calls & Praying for the Sick

If you are preaching an evangelistic message, in a church or in a campaign, it is essential to make an appeal for people to make a decision and to respond to the Gospel you have just preached. Different evangelists do this in slightly different ways. But let me share with you how I normally do this, and you can follow the same method. If you find a different way that works well for you, then that is absolutely fine.

You have now preached the Gospel and are going to give people a chance to respond and accept Jesus Christ as their Lord and Saviour. The first thing I would suggest is that you do not ask the worship team to come forward. This is common in many meetings and people mean well, they think they are creating a better atmosphere for the unsaved to respond to the Gospel. I can only say that in my opinion having a group of singers and musicians suddenly climbing the steps to the platform and picking up their instruments, at such a crucial time in the meeting, can be very distracting.

If you are preaching in a church, make sure you tell the pastor in advance that you would like to make an appeal. Ask him, or one of his assistants, to be at the back of the church during the appeal and to look and see who raises their hand. Often in a local church the pastor will know the people who raise their hands. He can then approach them after the meeting and offer to meet with them and give them some guidance on the first steps in the Christian life. Pastors will not usually think of doing this unless I ask them. In my home church one of the pastors goes to the back when I ask the congregation to bow their heads in prayer, after I have finished my message. He knows that I am about to make an appeal, so he goes to the back and watches to see who responds.

Ask people to bow their heads and to close their eyes for just a minute. Tell them that you want to give an opportunity to people who have never asked Jesus into their hearts to do so right now. If you are speaking in a church tell them that you are not going to embarrass them, point them out or bring them to the front. Now say: "Everyone here today who wants to accept Jesus as your Lord and Saviour, please raise your hand right now. Let me just acknowledge it, then you can take it down again. I am the only person watching from the platform." NB: Never say: "Is there anyone here today who wants to accept Jesus as your Lord and Saviour?" Expect that there are people present who need to respond to the Gospel. As hands are raised say: "God bless you, I see your hand, thank you." This often encourages others who are sensing the conviction of the Holy Spirit to respond as well, they are not alone.

If you are preaching in a larger, open-air campaign the system I use is very similar. I usually ask people firstly to stand up. Usually in an open-air campaign meeting some people will be sitting and others will be standing. I ask everyone to stand up, to close their eyes and to bow their heads. The fact that they are standing makes it easier when I later invite those who respond to come to the front. I ask that nobody moves around for the next few minutes. I then follow the same steps which I have outlined in the point above. Once I see many hands raised in the air I usually say: "Oh it is wonderful to see so many hands being raised and people wanting to accept Jesus as their Saviour tonight!" I then ask everyone who raised their hand to come to the area we always keep clear in front of the platform.

The next step is to lead people in the prayer of salvation. In a church I will ask the whole church to repeat this prayer out loud, sentence by sentence after me. In an open-air campaign meeting I give people a few minutes to come to the area at the front of the platform. Usually I ask the local interpreter to lead the prayer of salvation and tell the people to repeat what he says, in a loud voice, sentence by sentence. If the interpreter is not a pastor, or not confident in doing this, I will ask a local senior pastor to do this. This makes it less complicated than having me pray, then having the interpreter pray, and then finally the people praying each sentence.

The Prayer of Salvation

Here is an example of the prayer of salvation I would often use, the dots indicate a pause after each phrase or sentence: *"Lord Jesus Christ...thank you for dying for me on the cross...I am sorry for my sins...I believe that You are the Son of God...I believe You took the punishment for my sins on the cross...I believe that You rose again from the dead...Come into my heart today...take away my sins...make me a new person...I am now a believer in Jesus Christ... Help me to live for You...from this day forward...I ask You to protect me...I ask You to give me eternal life after I die...Thank You Jesus... In Your name I pray...Amen."*

I then give people three simple pieces of advice. (1) Start to pray to God every day in the name of Jesus. (2) Start to read the Bible every day, starting in the New Testament. (3) Get involved in a local church that believes the Bible and preaches from it.

In our campaigns we usually give people who come forward a copy of the Gospel of John in the local language. In church meetings I always bring with me some paperback New Testaments and a simple booklet that explains the first steps in the Christian life. Usually the pastor will give these to people whom he has seen raise their hands during the salvation appeal.

Praying for the sick

This is a huge subject. I could easily write a whole book just on this topic alone. However, that is not the main purpose of this book. So let me give you some key points to help you in ministering to the sick as a guest evangelist in a church, or in an open-air Gospel campaign.

In both churches and in my campaigns, I normally pray one prayer over the whole church or crowd. I don't normally pray for people one at a time. There is absolutely nothing wrong in doing that, and many people minister to the sick that way, especially in churches where there are fewer people. In open-air campaigns we usually have big crowds, and many people want prayer for healing. It is therefore not practical to pray for one person at a time, we would be there for many hours, and it is just not practical to minister that way.

In a church situation, I simply ask people who want prayer for healing to place one hand on their heart, as a simple sign of faith. I then tell them that I am going to pray a simple prayer for healing in the name of Jesus. I ask people to expect something to happen as I pray. I then pray a prayer over the congregation, commanding all sickness, pain, and disease to leave the people, in the name of Jesus Christ. I then ask people to check themselves, during the closing worship, and to see what God has done in their bodies. I ask people to come and tell me afterwards what has happened, or to tell one of the pastors. Often, we hear some great healing testimonies of what God has done.

In our open-air campaigns I ask those who are sick to come to the front of the platform. Usually a large number of people come forward in Africa and Asia. I encourage them to expect something to happen when I pray for them. Often, I will quickly share a healing testimony from a previous evening, just to try and encourage them in their faith. Sometimes I tell them briefly about the lady who pushed through a crowd and touched the hem of Jesus' garment and received her healing. I encourage them to copy her simple faith.

In our campaigns we always have a large team of uniformed volunteers working with us. They record the names and addresses of people who give their lives to Jesus each night for future follow up by local pastors. I instruct the volunteers to help me as I pray from the platform. I ask them to move through the crowd and lay their hands on as many heads possible. I tell them to simply say: "In the name of Jesus Christ be healed!"

I then start to pray a strong prayer commanding every sickness and pain to leave the people. It is very important to boldly take authority in the name of Jesus Christ. Never pray "If it be your will," that is the prayer of consecration, what is needed here is the prayer of faith. I also command evil spirits to leave the people, in Africa and Asia many people are troubled and even possessed by demonic spirits. Sometimes people will start to clearly manifest the presence of an evil spirit. They usually begin to shake violently and to start shouting loudly and uncontrollably. Some of the volunteers will then carry them out of the crowd to an area behind the platform where local pastors will pray for their deliverance. It is important that such people are removed quickly from the crowd, or they will cause a lot of disturbance.

Praying for Healing

Here is an example of the type of prayer for healing I would normally pray in a campaign meeting. I will pause after each phrase, so the interpreter can repeat what I have said: *"Almighty God, we come to you now in the name of your Son Jesus Christ. Thank you that Jesus died and rose again from the dead for our sins. Thank you that there is power in the name of Jesus Christ to heal us and to deliver us. I take authority in the name of Jesus Christ over every sickness and disease attacking people here today. I command every sickness and every evil spirit to go in the name of Jesus Christ! I command headaches to go. I command blind eyes to see and deaf ears to open. I command people to be healed in the back, in the heart and in the stomach. I command lame legs to be healed in the name of Jesus Christ! I rebuke every sickness and disease in the name of Jesus and command them to leave the people now! I bind every evil spirit attacking people here tonight. I command them to leave the people in the name of Jesus Christ! I proclaim healing in this place tonight in the name of Jesus. Let miracles happen now in the name of Jesus Christ, the Son of the Living God. Lord, we thank you for healing people tonight, we thank you for setting people free from evil spirits tonight. We give you all the praise and all the glory, in Jesus' name, amen."*

After I have finished my prayer, I then tell people to check themselves and to see what God has done. I tell people who had a sore arm to start to move their arm. I tell people who came with a friend who was deaf to check his hearing etc. I also ask the volunteers to ask individual people what has happened, how are they feeling now? I ask the volunteers to bring people who have definitely received their healing to the steps at the side of the platform. A small team of our local leaders and pastors are there and will speak to the person and carefully verify that the healing is real and genuine. We then allow some of the most dramatic cases to come up onto the platform and to give a testimony.

Once someone comes onto the platform to testify to healing, I will conduct a short interview with them. I usually ask them what was wrong with them? Then I ask what happened when we prayed this evening? Then I try to get them to demonstrate their healing in a visible way. For example, if someone says their back is healed, I will ask them to bend their back several times. If someone had a lame leg or painful knees, I ask them to run around the platform. Finally I will ask them who has healed them? I always make sure that they say that it is Jesus Christ who has healed them.

These healing testimonies are very important in an evangelistic campaign, especially in countries where a different religion is dominant. The healings prove to people that the Gospel message we have preached about Jesus is true. The Bible says in Mark Chapter 16 verse 20 (NKJV): *"And they went out and preached everywhere, the Lord working with them and confirming the word through the accompanying signs."* Healing testimonies also attract more people to come the next night and therefore more people will hear the Gospel. I remember a teacher at the Bible School I attended many years ago telling us, "Healings and miracles are God's PR method!" There is certainly truth in that saying. On some occasions we have started a campaign with a very small crowd. But as people are healed and give testimonies, we nearly always see the crowd grow rapidly night after night.

Read what the Bible says about divine healing. Study the ministry of Jesus and the disciples as they ministered to sick people. Read faith building books about healing written by people who believe that the Lord heals today and who are seeing results in their own lives and ministries. There are many excellent books on the subject, but I will just recommend two to you now: "Healing the Sick" by T. L. Osborn and "Christ the Healer" by F. F. Bosworth, both should be readily available online. T. L. Osborn was a great campaign evangelist who held huge campaigns in Africa and Asia, he saw many miracles of healing in his meetings. F. F. Bosworth conducted evangelistic and healing campaigns across the USA, his book is considered a classic on divine healing.

A lady tells Richard that her back has been healed

Richard ministering to people in Kenya.

Chapter 11

"Top Tips for Travellers!"

There are a number of things I have learned over many years of travelling, especially by air. I am still learning and picking up tips myself! But here are some things that might help you.

- Try to book flights etc. well in advance, so that you get the best choice and deals. Try to book a ticket with some flexibility, if it is not too expensive, just in case your plans have to be changed.

- I like to book my seat well in advance and always prefer an aisle seat. You don't want to be allocated a centre seat by the airline, with total strangers either side of you, on a long distance, overnight flight.

- Check well in advance that your passport is valid and has a minimum of six months on it, after the date you return home from your trip. Make sure you allow a long time to apply for any visa you may need, this can often take a long time to process and get your passport back to you.

- If you are going to be travelling a lot, ask your national passport agency if you can have a second passport. Some countries will issue a second passport to frequent travellers on request. This is very useful if you are waiting a long time for a visa but need to travel again whilst the first passport is away.

- Always pay with a credit card, never with a debit card. This gives you far more protection and a much higher chance of getting your money back if something goes wrong. If an online travel agency is not refunding money, which you believe you are entitled to, then contact your credit card company for help.

- If possible, try to book directly with the airline, rather than with an agency. Again, you will probably get more help from an airline if something goes wrong, or a flight is cancelled, than from an online agency.

- Always allow yourself plenty of time at the airport, and between flights if you have to transfer on the way.

- If it is on offer at the airport you will fly from, then book "fast track security." This is often cheap but can save you a lot of time waiting in a line for security checks at an airport. I often do this at Dublin Airport which I frequently use. It only costs a few Euros, and I also get a free coffee with the fast-track ticket!

- Enrol in a lounge programme with "Priority Pass." This will give you access to business lounges at most airports, even when you are flying in economy. The more basic programmes they offer allow you to pay each time you use a lounge. I only use my card if I have more than three hours between flights, otherwise I just use the regular departure lounge facilities. Lounges usually offer free food, drinks coffee etc, so you can often actually save money, despite paying a lounge entry fee to "Priority Pass."

- Enrol in any loyalty programmes with airlines you use and register the relevant card number every time you fly with that airline.

- Travel light! Don't bring too much luggage with you. If at all possible, try to avoid checking in a suitcase. This will save you a lot of time standing in a queue to check in your suitcase, also on arrival waiting for it to be delivered to the baggage belt. If you have a short connection time between two flights, there is a high risk your suitcase will not be transferred to the next flight in time by the airline. I very rarely check in a suitcase and find I can manage fine with hand luggage only.

- You should normally be able to pack everything you will need into a cabin size roller suitcase, plus a lap top size bag. You are normally allowed a reasonable amount of cabin baggage on long distance flights. Carefully check the size and weight you are allowed to bring on board and be sure to follow that particular airline's limits. Some airlines will spot check hand luggage and charge you quite a large fee, if you have exceeded their weight or size guidelines for hand luggage.

- If you must check in a larger suitcase, make sure you have some spare clothes, your notes, toiletries, chargers, and any other essentials in your hand luggage, just in case your suitcase is lost or delayed along the way.

- Try to mark any black suitcases in some way, so that they look distinct and different, many people use black suitcases. I have a black roller suitcase, but I have added bright blue strips of a strong tape to the sides, this avoids it getting mixed up with another passenger's luggage or being lifted in error by someone else. I also have a large, orange luggage label on my case, to make it stand out.

- Make sure your luggage is clearly marked with your name and contact number. My son puts a small tracker inside his suitcase, if it gets lost at least he knows exactly where it is and can track it on his phone.

- Don't bring too many clothes with you. If you run out of clothes, just wash some in soap and water in the wash basin or shower in the hotel room. If you hang the wet clothes neatly on coat hangers, they will usually be dry by the following morning in a hotter climate.

- Try to bring clothes which have polyester in them, they are much less likely to crease than clothes made of 100% cotton. They will also dry quickly.

- Make sure you have a good travel insurance policy, this is vital!

- Plan well ahead and allow yourself good time and your trip should be relatively stress free!

- Always cover your trip and all your luggage with prayer before you set off, this is very important! Ask the Lord to protect you and your luggage every step of the way.

Staying healthy in other countries....

Here are a few tips about how to stay healthy when travelling to other countries, especially in Africa and Asia.

- Speak to your doctor in advance, get his advice on vaccinations, malaria tablets etc.

- Make sure you have a good travel insurance policy from a reputable company. Make sure the country to which you are travelling is covered by the policy.

- Take malaria tablets, if they have been prescribed for you by your doctor.

- Use a mosquito net, if one is provided in your hotel room.

- Spray your bedroom with insect spray a couple of hours before going to bed.

- Don't drink tap water, buy bottled water and make sure the cap is sealed when you open it.

- Don't ask for ice cubes in your drinks, they have probably been made using tap water.

- Be careful what you eat. Make sure hot food is really hot or freshly cooked. Avoid foods which you suspect have been kept warm for a long time, warm temperatures are the ideal breeding ground for bacteria. Avoid salads and ice cream and other dairy products.

- Foods which you peel yourself are normally safe to eat e.g. bananas and other fruits. Anything that comes in a sealed package, a bottle, or a tin is also usually safe to eat.

- Don't feel you have to eat something, just because it has been served to you. If you get sick, you will possibly not be able to preach and do the job you came to do.

- Try to sleep and eat in hotels and restaurants which are of a reasonable standard, as far as this is possible.

Staying safe in other countries....

Here are some quick tips about how to stay safe when travelling to other countries, especially in Africa and Asia..

- Claim God's protection over yourself, your colleagues, and all your possessions and property, each morning and at night before sleeping

- Carefully follow all advice given to you by your local contact, respect their requests.

- Keep your valuables with you at all times, especially your passport and credit cards.

- Be very cautious about buying anything from a street seller. Things such as mobile phones, watches, designer label clothes etc. are probably fake.

- Don't go out alone at night, unless your contact has clearly told you it is safe to do so.

- Make sure you know the room numbers and mobile numbers of your contact and others travelling with you.

- Don't open the door of your hotel room at night, without first asking who is there.

- Only change money at a bank or an official "bureau de change," never on the street.

Chapter 12

Questions & Answers

In this section Richard answers a number of questions which have been put to him recently by Bible School students and other young people.

Q. How many sermons do you have that you use regularly?

A. I have many sermons that I have written since I first started in ministry in 1990. Some I have used many times in various campaigns and church outreach meetings. Others I have only used once or twice, and then never used again. As each campaign in Africa and Asia is in a different town, with new people attending, I tend to use the same few sermons over and over again. They are all featured in this book. I use these ones firstly because I like them, and also because they are proven soul winners; as the title of this book says they are "Evangelistic Sermons That Work!" I keep a written record of every sermon I preach, where and when I preached it. In this way I don't use the same sermon in the same place twice. I also keep all my paper outlines in files and my PowerPoints on a memory stick.

Q. What are the most common mistakes young people make when preaching?

A. I have regularly had young preachers accompany me on mission trips, and I often give them opportunities to preach. The biggest mistakes are covered in many of the things I have mentioned in Chapters 7 and 8 in this book. Often young preachers do not have a clear line of thought in their preaching, they tend to jump around with no clear structure. I have written clearly about all these things in this book.

Secondly, there is often a failure to vary the speed and level of their voice when preaching. Thirdly, there is a failure to use illustrations, or to share a personal example from their own lives, to help illustrate the point they are trying to make.

Q. Is it important to have your own style when preaching?

A. Yes, it is absolutely vital to preach in your own style. Don't try to copy famous preachers. You can certainly learn from them but don't copy their style, be yourself! You are unique, your DNA and fingerprints are different from everyone else on this earth. There is only one you, so don't be afraid to be yourself and preach in a way that you feel comfortable with. I believe that there are certain principles which you can follow which will help you, I have outlined them in this book, but definitely be yourself and develop your own style.

Q. If you could go back in time and give advice to your younger self as a young preacher, what advice would you give?

A. That is great question. I would probably tell my younger self two things: Spend more time reading your Bible and spend more time in prayer. Both those things sound very simple and basic, and they are. But looking back I think I should have spent more time in prayer and Bible reading than I did as a young preacher. We are told in Acts Chapter 6 verse 4 (NKJV) the disciples told the early church: *"We will give ourselves continually to prayer and to the ministry of the word."*

As I have got older, I have realised, more and more, the importance of prayer, both individually and corporately. The more we pray the more results we will see, both individually and in our churches. I have also come to appreciate even more, how important it is to regularly read the Bible. That is where faith comes from, as we are told in Romans Chapter 10 verse 17 (NKJV): *"So then faith comes by hearing and hearing by the word of God."* Faith does not come from praying, although it is good and right to pray much, faith comes from the word of God. As you read it, believe it, speak it, and act upon it then your faith will grow and develop.

Q. You have been travelling quite a lot over the past 32 years. How did you keep a balance between ministry, family, and your personal relationship with God?

A. I have always had three priorities in life, especially since I got married in 1988. They are as follow: (1) My relationship with God comes first, He has to be number 1 (2) My relationship to my wife comes second, closely followed by my relationship with my three sons. (3) My relationship to my ministry and the work God has called me to do comes third, not first. This means that if my wife and family need me for something important and the ministry also needs me, then I will put my wife and family first. I found that having these clear priorities has helped me to keep a balance in my life and ministry.

Q. I feel God is calling me to go and do campaigns in Africa and Asia, as you have been doing for many years, but how do I get started?

A. The first thing I would recommend you do is to get some kind of training. Before I started preaching, I attended a Bible

College in Norway for one year. It was a school very much focused on mission and evangelism, rather than pastoral ministry. If that is not possible for you, maybe you can study some kind of course online that is relevant to your calling, provided by a ministry or college with a similar vision to your own.

Secondly, try to join a short-term campaign team which is going to Africa or Asia to hold a campaign. You will probably only need money for your airfare and personal expenses. The evangelists in our network ACE (Association of Campaign Evangelists) are always willing to give opportunities to young people who feel they have a calling. Often, we let young preachers do a "warm up," a short message for five minutes before the evangelist preaches. This will give you a feel for what it is like to preach in such meetings, then you can better decide if this is for you or not. For more details please visit the ACE website www.ace-evangelists.org

Q. As a young person, how do I get the money I need to travel and preach the Gospel?

A. When we first started in ministry, as missionaries to Kenya, we wrote to all our friends and family and friends in church. We asked them if they would consider supporting us for six months or giving a once only donation. Many people did respond and agreed to give a monthly donation for six months, others gave a single donation. You will find that people are happy to support a young person with a vision and who is planning to do something for God. But if you just sit at home and say, "I have no money," then nothing will happen. It is when you start to move that things start to happen.

As money starts to come in, I would encourage you to give 10% (a tithe) away to another person or ministry with a similar vision. I have done this for many years and always found that the Lord has been faithful to meet our needs and inspire the right person to give at the right time. Jesus said in Luke Chapter 6 verse 38 (NKJV): *"Give and it will be given to you."* Many times this is overlooked. We want to fund raise, pray, rebuke the devil etc. and there is nothing wrong with any of those things, there is a time and a place for all of them. But Jesus plainly tells us that if we will give first, then it will be given to us by other people. This is where faith comes into the picture, you have to take a step of faith and give out of what you have, trusting God to respond and meet your own needs as you give to meet the needs of others. It is very true to say: "Your needs are not met according to what other people give to you, your needs are met according to what you give to other people." Read that a few times and then think about it carefully.

Q. What weapons does the devil use to try and attack young preachers?

A. There are two things in particular with which you need to be very careful, money and sex. Many great preachers have fallen and lost their ministry due to mistakes in one of these two areas of life.

Money: As money starts to come into your ministry make sure every donation is carefully recorded, also keep a detailed record of every payment. You may need to employ an accountant to help you with this and to set up a proper system. Keep all money that comes in for your ministry in a separate account to your own personal finances. Make sure you follow all the rules and regulations of the country you live in. Be totally honest and open with money and make sure everything is properly accounted for.

I would suggest that you always be sure to thank every person who gives to your ministry, it is best to do this by email or by post. Don't just send some impersonal message but address the person by name. Tell them you really appreciate their support and how you plan to use their gift. If you send them a letter, make sure you sign it personally. People like to feel appreciated and to know that their gift has arrived safely, these things are important.

Remember, the people who support you financially are your partners and "co-workers" in the Gospel, not just names on a mailing list. There are three types of missionaries, "foot" missionaries who get to go and preach, "knee" missionaries who pray for the foot missionaries, and finally there are "hand" missionaries who put their hand in their pocket and give financially to support the foot missionaries. All are equally important and worthy in God's sight. Make sure your "knee and hand" missionaries know that they are appreciated by you.

Sex: Be extremely careful in your relations and contacts with people of the opposite sex. Avoid even the appearance of anything that could possibly be viewed by another person as suspicious of being immoral. Let me give you some examples of how I approach these things. I would never travel alone on a mission trip with a single lady unless my wife, or some other people were with me. It just would not look right. If I am staying in a hotel and a lady member of staff comes to my door to clean my room, I always step out of the room until she has finished. Never get involved in privately praying for a person of the opposite sex unless someone else is with you. Don't give anyone a single opportunity to accuse you of anything wrong or immoral. Paul told the Thessalonians in 1st Thessalonians Chapter 5 verse 22 (KJV) to *"Avoid every appearance of evil."*

Even if something is perfectly innocent, it may have an "appearance of evil" in the eyes of someone else. Preachers of the Gospel need to maintain the highest possible standards in all of these things.

Q. Have you made any mistakes that younger preachers can learn from?

A. I think as a young leader I was sometimes too hard on people in certain situations. There is a fine line to walk in life as a leader between being too hard and being too soft. I think in some situations as a younger leader I should have not been so hard on some people in certain situations. As I look back over my life and ministry, I wish I had been gentler in some situations.

Q. You have been in full time ministry for over 32 years, was it worth it?

A. The answer to that question is undoubtedly "yes!" It has not always been easy, there have been many struggles and difficulties, as well as many successes. There have been times when we have faced great opposition. There have been times when we have had a lot of money in the ministry, but there have been times when we have had nothing and have had to really trust the Lord to provide for us. There have been times when we have seen great success and blessing, and other times when things did not seem to go well. There have been times when our faith has been greatly tested, and it looked like nothing was happening. But any negatives have been far outweighed by the joy of seeing many thousands come to the Lord, people being physically healed, and many churches planted. You can read more about all these things in my book, "From Belfast to the Ends of the Earth!" which you can buy on

Amazon, it tells you my life story up to the present day. Would I do it all again? Absolutely, yes!

God bless you as you preach and teach the word of God!

Richard Gunning
Northern Ireland, May 2023

Richard Gunning and his interpreter leading
hundreds to Jesus in Burkina Faso.

To find out more...

To find out more about Richard Gunning and the work of Reach the Unreached Ministries (RTU) and the Association of Campaign Evangelists (ACE) then please visit our websites.

www.rtuministries.co.uk

www.ace-evangelists.org

Find us on Facebook: @rtuministries

Donate:
To donate to the work of RTU Ministries just visit the website and then click on DONATE. This will bring you to a secure page where you can donate by credit/debit card or by PayPal.

www.rtuministries.co.uk

If you prefer to send a cheque, please make it payable to "RTU Ministries" and post it to our head office: RTU Ministries, 2 Belair Park, Newtownards BT23 4UX, Northern Ireland, UK.

Invite:
To invite Richard Gunning to speak in your church or outreach event, please email us at office@rtuministries.co.uk. Money is not a condition, and every invitation is prayerfully considered.

Newsletter:
To receive our free monthly newsletter, by post or by email, please email us at office@rtuministries.co.uk

Read:

To buy a copy of Richard Gunning's life story, **"From Belfast to the Ends of the Earth!"** please go to your preferred Amazon site and enter the title in the search bar.

Becoming a Christian:

To find out more about how to become a Christian and the first steps in following Jesus, just download the app
"New Life School"
https://app.nlschool.com/
(This app is free of charge)

The Association of Campaign Evangelists (ACE),
founded in 2002 by Richard Gunning.

Endorsements

Richard Gunning has a unique ministry, I know of no other like it in Ireland or the UK. He is called by God as an evangelist, church planter and leader of men. I have personally known Richard for many years and our church happily partners with him in this great work. Richard is a man of integrity and a mature servant of the Lord, he is a blessing to the fivefold ministry and the body of Christ.

Pastor David Goudy
Moira Pentecostal Church, Northern Ireland

Having seen the ministry of Richard Gunning and RTU Ministries first hand and since its beginning, I have always been impressed by the founders, Richard and Agnes Gunning. They are people of integrity, faithfulness, and honesty. They have shown complete dedication to the cause of Christ over many years, and I cannot recommend them highly enough.

Paul Reid
Pastor Emeritus, Christian Fellowship Church, Belfast,
Northern Ireland

Richard Gunning has a unique gift to inspire others, like me, to serve the Lord even more zealously! I personally do not know anyone else who stretches his faith so generously for the sake of others development in ministry. I have seen over the years how God has used Richard to raise up new evangelists and develop strategies to reach whole states and regions with the Gospel of Jesus Christ.

Rickard Lundgren
Founder of Go Out Mission, Sweden

Richard Gunning's worth to the Kingdom of God has been truly significant. I have known him for over twenty years as he has ministered in our church, and as we have travelled together to the mission fields of Kenya and Burkina Faso. Richard, through Reach the Unreached Ministries, has certainly helped transform hundreds of thousands of lives along the way for God's glory.

Pastor Jonathan R. Payne
Senior Minister, Ballymoney Church of God, Northern Ireland

Reach the Unreached Ministries (RTU) is a highly effective organisation, passionately and diligently pursuing the Great Commission, committed to bringing the Gospel to all nations. Richard Gunning is a driven and inspiring leader who is relentless and faithful to the call of God on his life. I have no hesitation in urging you to partner in the amazing work carried out by RTU Ministries.

Stephen Stewart
Northern Ireland businessman and supporter of RTU Ministries

Printed in Great Britain
by Amazon

34275308R00096